TIM NEVE

Photography by Johan Palsson

INTERIORS
INSPIRED BY THE COAST

SANDCASTLES

MURDOCH BOOKS

Foundations of Style

THE WORD SANDCASTLES
CONJURES UP MEMORIES OF CHILDHOOD HOLIDAYS, DON'T YOU THINK?

Building sandcastles is a wonderful activity: no two castles are ever the same; each pile of sand is crafted uniquely and takes on an aesthetic that, perhaps, reflects the sculptor's personality. The most exciting part is the final decoration, a little like icing a cake but, in this case, the finishing touch might be a special shell or drape of seaweed to mark the design as one's own.

Such a metaphor seemed fitting on my journey to make this book, visiting homeowners who had created their own 'sandcastles'. Each home was close to, or inspired by, the shore and paid homage to the sea. What quickly emerged was how different they could be, from a revamped 1940s caravan on the water's edge in Frankston, Victoria, to a tepee structure in the laidback town of Bangalow, New South Wales. All lovingly created and cared for by their owners as their unique take on coastal style.

So, the question might be: if you were given time to sit in the sand and play, what kind of castle would you build to call home?

I had been working as a magazine stylist for a couple of years when my own coastal home was featured in *Real Living* interiors magazine. The article was such a success that I pitched the idea to my publishers to feature a series of similar homes. Photographer Johan and I travelled up and down the glorious eastern Australian coastline, capturing the style on film. That series instigated a whirlwind of positive reader feedback and, now that we had built up a portfolio, I suggested to the publishers that we launch a national title. *Australian Coastal Home* magazine was born.

It was wonderful to be the founder of something fresh and new. Personal passion had translated into a magazine that became an instant success with readers and I spent the next two years editing seven seasonal issues of *Australian Coastal Home* before embarking on my next publishing venture.

Foundations of style

WHEN YOU HEAR THE PHRASE COASTAL DECORATING I DON'T BLAME YOU IF YOU SHUDDER. FOR TOO LONG FAUX STARFISH AND MASS-PRODUCED GONE FISHIN' SIGNS HAVE REIGNED SUPREME AND MUDDIED THE WATERS OF WHAT SHOULD BE THE CLEAREST, MOST AUTHENTIC, INSPIRATION IN HOME STYLING.

This book aims to return the style to its purest form and to develop a once-clichéd decorating mode into further sister-styles. There's a true difference between tropical and nautical, bohemian and beach, as you'll see in the following chapters, each of which reveals a different take on the core inspiration.

Each chapter acts as a stand-alone interpretation of modern coastal style. You might find you are drawn towards one particular aesthetic, or perhaps two or three. Notice how each uses a different palette; sometimes the variations are subtle but all are inspired by ocean lifestyles.

Those different aesthetics were apparent to me while I was working on this book. By moving from one beachside locale to another I uncovered a distinct sense of modern coastal style. We took inspiration from the balmy tropics of northern Queensland, down to the serene fishing villages of Tasmania, and everything we discovered in between. We travelled the east coast, the playground of my early family holidays – I love revisiting those places with adult eyes. Like so many people, I have enduring memories of those family holidays, packed into a car with siblings, on the long road trip to the endless summer beach vacation. Just the mention of those place names conjures up their own unique personalities: Byron Bay brings to mind a bohemian spirit, as opposed to the formal residences of Sydney's northern beaches, or the colourful European-style beach shacks of Melbourne. These instant place memories occur in all parts of the world... Consider a pebbly English beach, perhaps with a wave-lashed pier and a traditional seafaring culture, then contrast that with the classic aesthetic that comes to mind at the mention of the Hamptons in the USA, or the paint colours of the vibrant Italian coast.

It's not all about feeling the salt on your skin, either. A large part of my work as editor of *Australian Coastal Home* magazine was reminding readers that you didn't need coastal views to embrace the carefree aesthetic the seaside inspires. The magazine illustrated the point with real home tours in far-flung locations. This is a theme I have hoped to continue with this book. It might be hard to believe, but our first photo shoot location was a converted dairy farm four hours from the coast. There's a good chance that in such a remote country town some of the younger inhabitants might not even have seen the ocean. However, as a self-confessed sea-lover it was as far inland as I have ever travelled. It was a real eye-opener to discover that the same tranquillity I love about the coast can also be found on an isolated country property. I'm fairly confident you won't be able to label this inland house from the photographs, which is proof that effortless coastal style can be achieved anywhere, no matter which plot or pavement you might call home.

Another aim is to show that the coastal aesthetic can be embraced all year round. With our enviable climate, we've become experts at blending seamless indoor and outdoor living: it suits our weather forecast, no matter which month. For those in cooler climates, take heart that within any four walls you can easily evoke a warmer season and be transported there. Dazzle and confuse the senses with carefully selected furnishings and a sunnier paint tone than is on offer outside.

The whole idea of an interior design book like this is to make you think about your personal tastes and approach to creating your home and its spaces. What I didn't count on is that writing the book would make me question my own interior aesthetic and design choices. By testing out different looks in our 'temporary style laboratories' on location, I discovered many new things. I encourage you to do the same.

MY COASTAL ANCESTRY

You could say interiors are in my blood. My not-too-distant ancestors were early furniture retailers in my hometown of Newcastle, New South Wales. My great great grandfather, Walter Neve, owned a series of shops with grand-sounding names, such as 'The Neve Great Northern Furniture Bazaar' and 'Reliable Home Furnishers'. I like to imagine he was a Mr Selfridge of sorts, imparting interior style to the masses. Sepia photos from the early twentieth century (not only from our family archives but also historical cityscapes in local newspapers) are evidence of shops, workshops and warehouses in numerous locations, all with the Neve name proudly displayed. An advertisement shows the range of ornate pieces he offered, from sea grass lounge suites to satin cushions.

Walt had an interest in the coast, as testified by his business card: 'Cabins refitted and ships' furnishing generally promptly attended to.' A further link to the sea is far sadder: Walter was found drowned on Newcastle Beach in 1907. The *Sydney Morning Herald* of December 30 announced:

One of the oldest and most respected citizens of Newcastle was carried out and drowned before help could reach him. As had been his daily custom for many years, he went onto the beach for his daily dip. The late Mr Neve, 66, was one of the oldest of Newcastle's citizens, having resided here for 41 years. He was universally respected as one of the most honourable and upright of men.'

Archives show the Neve family business was sold to a bigger, national company in 1937. How I wish it had been kept in the family; I would have proudly taken the reins when my time came.

It is interesting to remember that coastal property was once very unfashionable. In the early twentieth century cheap residences were often constructed on the shoreline, where the sandy soil was not desirable. Generations later, beach culture, ocean views and better transport have changed this perspective.

In Civic Park, Newcastle's main public park, there is an anchor. When I was a child, my dad would take me there and tell how his father had worked with the Naval Association and helped place that anchor as a permanent landmark. That grandfather even had his ashes scattered in the sea off Newcastle. My family's anchor has always been dropped in my hometown – with such strong ties I guess that's why I'll always call Newcastle my home, and why I have such an enduring connection to the sea.

Walter Neve

GREAT NORTHERN FURNISHING BAZAAR,

80 Hunter Street, Newcastle

CABINS REFITTED AND SHIPS' FURNISHING GENERALLY PROMPTLY ATTENDED TO.

Your Order will be esteemed.

Walter Neve's Great Northern Furniture
Bazaar, around 1912.

Easy Chair, adjustable back. Upholstered in tapestry 45/-

Mobile Trays, with folding tops,
47/6.

Student's Table, with drawer and
book-shelves 42/6

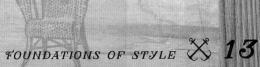

TAKING AN INSPIRED APPROACH

More often than not, I go with gut instinct, something that just 'feels right', when I am styling an interior. I'm drawn to the unexpected solution too, but I guess that's part of the job description – always looking for the most unique option.

However, in an effort to explain my approach here I've had to analyse my process more closely and have come to realise that my styling solutions are usually more temporary than permanent. I tend to encourage redecoration rather than renovation. It's a mantra I followed for over a decade as a property renter who had to work within someone else's boundaries. More recently, with the purchase of my first house, I've taken the same approach. I haven't rushed in and knocked down walls; instead, I opted for a quick coat of paint and an influx of decorative items to build a fresh look around my staple furniture pieces (that I always buy in neutral tones).

I'm also spontaneous; I like the idea that I can make over a room, simply on a whim, to suit my current mood or obsession. The favourite tools for such easy updates are paint (not only on walls, but also on furniture) and easily moveable objects such as one-off homewares and small furniture pieces.

I'm also increasingly drawn towards vintage items, especially those with an industrial edge. Pieces from another era ensure a point of difference as they are often unique (I like to avoid that 'off the shelf' look). Styling can even add functionality to such pieces, making them appear less decorative and perhaps more hard-working. Ropes and pulleys, for example, feature heavily throughout this book, styled with a sense of purpose to their surroundings. Overall, both vintage and industrial pieces usually offer a worn patina that suggests they have their own individual stories to tell.

From my magazine experience, I'm also familiar with encouraging readers to find the most cost-effective solutions on offer. By following such styling tactics you can adapt your home quickly to what is currently in vogue, if that's what you desire.

Above all, this 'temporary' approach most probably comes from my formal tertiary training in set and costume design. In theatre, all is mere impermanent scenery in make-believe worlds. Another aspect of modern theatre design is metaphor: suggestion reigns supreme. I'm always interested in what the items in a styled scenario suggest to an observer.

I recently heard a self-help guru advise that if you are ever lost in your career, go back to what you loved doing as a child. Find inspiration there, rather than in the grown-up concerns of money and status. How appropriate then that as a child I spent hours turning cardboard fridge boxes and masking tape into make-believe worlds inspired by the sets of my youth theatre group. The lesson here: never deny what truly inspires you.

HOW TO USE STYLED SCENARIOS

Throughout this book you'll notice that I refer to 'styled scenarios', 'settings' and 'schemes' rather than rooms. These are the set-ups I create to demonstrate the style of each chapter. It's important to realise that, as scenarios, these aren't intended to represent fully fledged interior styling throughout a home. They are usually set up in real homes but require no sense of purpose or logic. Rather, they are drawn from whimsy and aim to engage in an exploration of style.

In a way, these set-ups resemble the window displays I create for retailers I work with: perhaps a single chair, a side table, a backdrop of fabric or wallpaper and one single statement piece that come together as a group in a perfect balance of scale to tell a story. They demonstrate a heightened take on reality, a little like a fashion magazine editorial spread. It's not often you would lift a look straight from the glossy pages into your everyday wardrobe; if you did, you might end up going to work with a blown-out afro and no pants on... Instead, you take inspiration from the colours, textures and patterns demonstrated and, perhaps, pick and mix individual pieces to create your own look. In the same way, you might be encouraged here to translate the single chair into a family chaise sofa, for example. Looking at these ideas will be an individual process that unveils what you are inherently drawn to as your own style.

To take the idea a step further, these styled scenarios are akin to real-life pin boards. Like the mood boards at the start of each chapter, ideas on a pin board are brought to life in a setting of furniture and homewares. Each piece on the board represents a colour, texture or pattern you can expand on. By pinning and sticking fabric and moving small furniture items and one-off finds together, you get to see the effect in real time.

Find a corner of your home that you're happy to play in. Paint a section of the wall, hang something unexpected, stick samples or swatches against each other and analyse the effect. This way you can see what tickles your fancy before committing to an entire scheme.

In an otherwise 'dead space' of this house, left, we set up a mini-installation to test out a scheme. Seek out wallpaper prints that trick the eye with photo-realistic textures – the paper here replicates washed-out timber boards in driftwood tones. Why not use a chair as a side table? And place a rope reel in the scheme to see what its natural texture and tone add to the overall look. Notice how the warmth of the copper ship in the artwork pulls out the red tones in the wood of the classic bentwood chair? We hung an enamel tin pendant light low into the space – by having such lightbulb cords dropped low in each room you can easily unscrew your shade and try another, without even reaching for a ladder. A glass float adds the final nautical touch, balancing the ship iconography of the artwork. A vintage desk fan mixes in another era and metallic sheen, adding a sense of playfulness and movement.

Foundations of style

DISCOVERING YOUR VISUAL VOCABULARY

As you turn the pages of this book you'll discover it reads as a visual narrative, a running commentary on styling ideas and set-ups.

Inspired by the images, I invite you to imagine the impetus behind each styled scenario... How did the setting come to exist? What does it say to you? Does it conjure up memories? There are no wrong or right answers.

As my interpretations unfold, you'll discover that you too have a vocabulary to tap into. Listen to the first reaction you have to an image and you'll notice what language develops. Write down your instinctive thoughts, if that helps. From here, you'll be able to share what inspires you with friends and, even more importantly, with the homewares salesperson or paint specialist who will help you to create your own look.

FINDING INSPIRATION IN YOUR SURROUNDINGS

What holds inspiration for you?

If there's one thing I'm adamant about, it's that for modern coastal styling to be truly authentic the inspiration has to come from the source. In contrast, by simply looking at editorial shots in magazines and imitating the décor, all we end up with is a diluted variation on the initial theme.

So, if you're lucky enough to be close by, take a walk along the ocean shoreline. What do you find that can be collected as inspiration? These lengths of sand are prime spots to discover free textural swatches for your home: the pearly oyster tones of a washed-up shell; the sea- and sun-battered patina of driftwood; the spiky organic forms of sea life; the corroded rock faces bubbling into new forms.

Inspiration can come from anywhere, and can be both natural and constructed: consider the primary-coloured nautical iconography at a marina or weathered signage of a lifeguard station. How could each of these be reinterpreted in your home? In thinking about this, you'll come up with a unique styling solution that resonates honestly and far more strongly than a decorative item straight off the shelf of a shop.

If you don't have a nearby shoreline to explore, pull out photos and postcards from your favourite coastal getaways. What fond memories do these conjure up for you? And, once again, how could you use those elements that stand out for you to create a vibe of natural escape in your home?

In this book hopefully you'll find textural inspiration, perhaps in the close-ups of nautical pass-me-bys which, when examined, reveal much more than first met the eye.

For me, a constant source of inspiration is my daily swim in the ocean baths (you end up with less sand in your Speedos than at the beach). The Art Deco façade of Newcastle Ocean Baths turns every visit into an occasion. In my everyday styling work I seek to capture the fresh essence of the cool crisp ocean waters, especially as the seasons change. There is nothing that clears my mind better than a breath of coastal air or a dip in the sea.

This antique scientific bureau is an ideal furniture piece for curating your own shell museum. Label each drawer to group ocean-floor finds. The top becomes a perfect display shelf for some favourite pieces; their textures and tones mingle here to wonderful effect. Take inspiration from their colours and forms as the basis for an interior scheme.

MOOD BOARDS & COLOUR PALETTES

At the opening of each chapter in this book you'll find a textured mood board that visually communicates the scheme ahead. This 'cut and paste' process is a common building block of design, no matter what medium the artist works in. Ask any interior stylist how they begin the design process and they will invariably answer that the first vital tool is always the mood board.

This visual blueprint can be referred to throughout the design process – the success of a mood board lies in its magical ability to subliminally unveil your own taste and style.

Start by collecting visual scraps that appeal to you. These will often be clippings from magazines and photographs of other homes; but you can go a step further and become a bowerbird, gathering finds from nature and your everyday travels. Small objects that hold precious memories of your life journey will also reveal something personal. The real intrigue of a mood board is in the texture: this three-dimensional manifestation of a concept or collection is instantly appealing.

Your pieces can be curated in any form. Allocate a pin board in your home or office that you're likely to glance at often. Or use a journal that you can carry around and stick ideas into.

Don't be too precious. Collage pieces alongside each other because they appeal to you, hold memories for you, or perhaps because they clash yet charm, even though you don't know why!

Sometimes you might notice that, although you were drawn to some clippings and offcuts, they don't work together as you had hoped. That's OK: simply start a new pile and watch as a secondary board develops. That's exactly what happens in a couple of the chapters that follow: we found that one styling genre actually resulted in a few different looks.

Now, stand back and examine your mood board. What are the strongest elements? Are there any recurring features in your collection? Is there a particular colour that emerges as a constant? Look closely at the textures of your elements. What you'll uncover is an overall insight into what visually appeals to you. A successful mood board will also reveal what works in terms of a colour palette and the groupings that emerge from randomly collected images and items.

Patterns might appear through repetition of shapes. As in nature, like attracts like. When we begin to look for this visual significance in the random, thrown-together pile of 'things we like', we begin to understand what truly inspires us.

If it helps, as words pop into your mind when you look at your mood board, don't be afraid to scrawl these into the scheme too. In this way you begin to articulate your style and create that design vocabulary, helping to verbalise what you're seeking.

Once you've identified your own personal trends, the next step is to imagine how these might translate into reality. Trawl the internet, searching the keywords you've unveiled through your board and see what furniture pieces match your brief.

Visit hardware and decorator stores and start matching paint swatches and fabric samples to the colours, tones and textures of your collection. Add these to the board.

Something else to try: when you've bought sample pots to match your swatches, shake the cans well to make sure the pigment is thoroughly mixed, then take off all the lids, arrange them next to each other, paint-side-up, and take a snap. Your photograph will reveal your palette in a more appealing (and more colour-accurate) format than the store swatches.

Most importantly, as you shop and then create your interior, refer back to the mood board to confirm that each choice reflects the personal aesthetic you formed as your styling foundation.

As I put together the mood boards for this book, I realised that mine work best as table-top creations. They are simply too heavy to hang! Rather than images from magazines and paper paint swatches, I'm drawn to one-off objects and random three-dimensional pieces that I find on my travels. I combine these to see what emerges. There is no wrong or right method here, and you might find your mood boards are image based, and so lighter, and can be hung up on the wall to look at.

Notice how the baseboard (the board that a mood board is created on) often creates a solid background. The mood board grows layer by layer but always lets the background breathe by never fully covering it. The lesson here is to always start with an inspiring blank canvas, whether that is cork, wood, linen, hessian… I'm usually drawn to a natural-coloured, tactile basecloth, much like the sand that forms the backdrop of most coastal locations.

After the mood board in each chapter, a colour palette demonstrates tones that go together to make up a similar scheme. How you reinterpret that is up to you: by using it alongside fabric swatches; or matching paint pigments, or reworking a piece of furniture or creating a feature wall.

When you look at an image that appeals to you, notice how many colours make up the whole. By isolating a segment of each colour and pulling it out as a swatch, you can build a coherent palette. For the technically minded, you can use the eyedropper tool in Photoshop to select a pure pixel of colour from an image. The final collection will be your preferred palette and explain the appeal of the image you were drawn to in the first place.

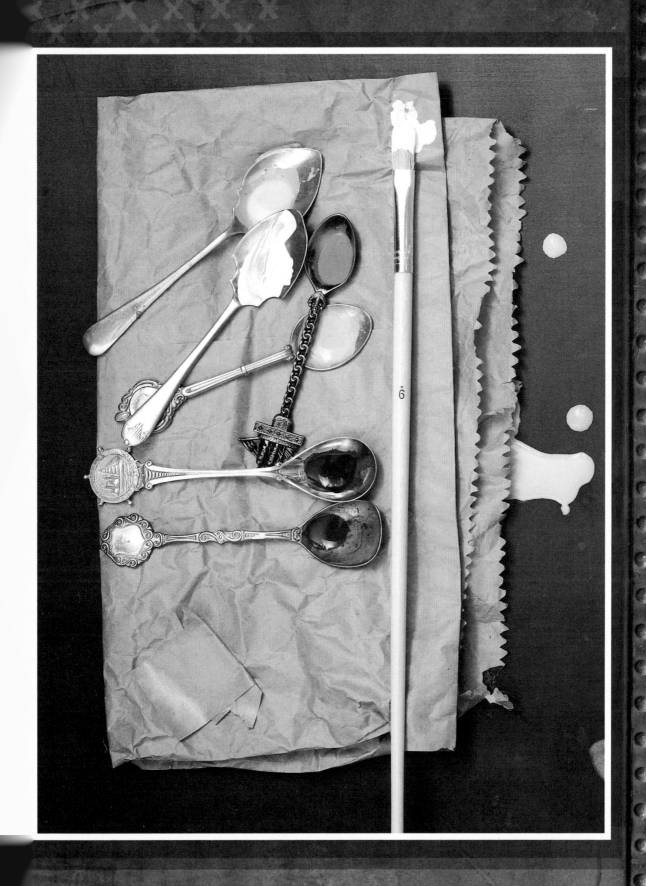

My dad's painting ladder and drop sheets with my decorative driftwood ladder, illustrating the combination of both of our skills and ideas in the creation of this book.

Dedication

Stephen Neve, 1955–2013

I was introduced to the wondrous effects of paint at a young age by my dad, Stephen. He was a professional house painter and ran a successful business for many decades. When I was a child, he came home from work every day splattered from head to toe, with dried paint in his hair and down his arms. The garage was always piled up with brushes, cans of paints and drop sheets.

If I try hard enough I might even remember the first time he showed me a fan deck of paint swatch cards, splitting open the pages to reveal the rainbow of colour choices that even just one company could offer.

My bedroom as a one-year-old might well have set my destiny. My mum, Rhonda, convinced Dad to buy a simple, untreated pine single bed and chest of drawers, but then he painted them vivid, glossy fire engine red. What a vision. It was proof of the ability of paint to create something completely unique and unlike any other piece of furniture in the world, just with a simple coat (or preferably two!) of paint.

I would never again have a simple bedroom set. As I grew up I was creating my own unique look on a constantly revolving basis. I consider this the best experimental training ever, and I thank my parents for giving me the freedom to do whatever I wanted, no matter how wild the idea. As a fourteen-year-old I explained to my local newspaper: 'I love art and hope to become an interior decorator. I practise this skill on my bedroom. I usually change it around every week. In the past month it has gone from modern silver to tribal African.' I guess it was no surprise that I would one day do the same professionally for other people.

Sadly, my father retired early due to illness, which recently claimed his life at a devastatingly young age. I have inherited the garage full of brushes, cans of paint and drop sheets, and they have been used wisely in the process of creating this book.

Whenever I pick up a paintbrush I will think of my father, and the passion for paint he has passed down to me as the next generation of our family.

Chapter 1

Beach comber

CELEBRATING THE NATURAL
SUNBLEACHED TONES AND SEA-WORN
TEXTURES OF SALVAGED TREASURES

THE WAVES FELL:
*WITHDREW AND FELL AGAIN, LIKE THE THUD
OF A GREAT BEAST STAMPING*

—THE WAVES, BY VIRGINIA WOOLF, 1931

Collecting inspiration

A walk along the shoreline can reveal a bounty of beautiful driftwood, shells and flotsam.

Smooth, wave-worn and faded, their exquisite natural forms beg us to lift them into a new life; driftwood, for example, can be transformed into practical interior focal points such as bedheads and coat racks. This is a salvaged look with an effortless air.

SUNDRENCHED
& SALT-BLEACHED

NATURAL AND NEUTRAL TEXTURES MINGLE ON THIS MOOD BOARD. Interwoven textiles are the main choices here, gathering in scale from fine hessian to open-weave basket cloth. The barely-there scheme is built up as a nest of natural matter, including tactile forms of a sea fan, sea sponges and shells of all shapes and sizes. Tones of brown-grey range from bark to whitewashed wood.

Beachcomber
(noun)

ONE WHO SCAVENGES ALONG BEACHES OR SHORE FOR ANYTHING OF WORTH; ESPECIALLY A VAGRANT LIVING ON THE SEASHORE.

BEACHCOMBER
COLOUR PALETTE

The wood textures here have been sandblasted and sundrenched until every fibre of colour has been stripped away. What is left is a naked colour palette of appealing sea-cleansed neutrals (1, 2, 3) that communicates a relaxed, unpretentious, laid-back vibe.

Picking the right neutral tone (4, 5) is difficult, especially in paint. As experience has probably taught you, a paint chip looks completely different under the fluorescent lights inside a store than in sunlight, so always buy a test pot – they're well worth the small expense – and paint different spots around your home. Watch how both natural daylight and artificial lighting affect the colour: neutrals can become garishly cream, throw a dirty grey or khaki tone or, worst of all, take on an unwanted pinkish hue.

SEEK OUT THESE ELEMENTS TO CREATE A BEACHCOMBER AESTHETIC IN YOUR HOME

➤ Seagull feathers ➤ Linen ➤ Driftwood ➤ Vintage books ➤ Sea-worn rope ➤ Hand-blown glass floats and bottles ➤ Coral, shells, dried seaweed, sea fans (all ethically collected) ➤ Sun hats ➤ Rugs in natural fibres, with raw edges ➤ Lobster pots and fishing nets ➤ Recycled timbers (especially atmospheric if reclaimed from once-working harbours) ➤ Maps ➤ Organic-shaped pottery, platters and vessels ➤ Raffia umbrellas ➤ Hessian sacks (to repurpose as floor cushions) ➤ Anything white (or that can be painted white) ➤ Palm fronds ➤ Brushed aluminium furniture ➤ Shutters and louvres

1

2

3

4

5

A NEUTRAL NEST

Some successful designers and stylists shoot to fame through their use of bold colour and pattern. My work was first noticed for the opposite: its lack of colour. In fact, it took me a while to shake off the term 'Mr Beige'. The nickname doesn't sound at all complimentary — beige being often used to describe the middle-of-the-road, boring option — but it became a life-changing thrill when my home was featured in *Real Living* interiors magazine under the headline 'Beige can be Beautiful'.

I had already been styling for magazines for a couple of years, but it was when I took the time to set up my own neutral nest that I found my aesthetic. The house was just a cheap rental property in my hometown of Newcastle, New South Wales, and it was cheap for good reason — the price was set to reflect its peeling paint and creaky floorboards. I negotiated a few weeks' waived rent when I told the agent I would update the rooms with a coat of neutral-coloured paint at my own expense.

The real inspiration for the interior design was the home's beachfront location. One weekend I found myself on the beach after a storm, greeted by washed-up remnants of driftwood and the sort of ocean treasures that only a stylist could be excited by. I arrived home with arms full of sticks and fronds for decorating and using as inspiration.

Neutral doesn't mean white. Some people love and long for all-white spaces, but I find that too blindingly bare. (Although I make an exception if the wall surfaces have texture: perhaps white-painted brickwork or tongue-and-groove wall panelling.)

THE PERFECT WHITE

I am often asked to define the 'perfect white' or the 'perfect neutral'. My thoughts are this:

Stark white is a good base to let neutrals sing. Make sure it has a serene blue hue rather than being too creamy-yellow.

For neutrals, I like a lingering combination of beige and grey tones, on the warmer side of muted mid-stone. I have fondly termed this colour 'greige'.

For my own home I went hunting for the perfect greige. I found a paint swatch that evoked a sense of bleached driftwood, somewhere between grey and beige, depending on the time of day and the amount of natural light. My greige worked well on the original Art Deco era walls — the imperfections of decades of wear and tear gave a delicate, plaster-feel to the colour.

The pure white trims and ceilings jumped out against the wall colour and freshened up the somewhat tired surfaces.

My choice for every thing in every room now followed this central palette of neutrals. Each selection was made interesting through the use of tactile fabrics and organically shaped decorations that worked with and against each other to create textured layers of interest.

I styled arrangements of these objects in any space I could: on the entry table; on open bathroom shelving; and on the original mantelpiece (a wonderful permanent shelf for decorating that I miss in my current, more modern, home. If you're lucky enough to have one, make the most of it). I used vintage fabrics, earthy vessels, paper and feathers; each collection told a visual story that added further interest.

A final touch in every room was an oversized, inexpensive pendant shade, hung low (I had ultra-high Art Deco ceilings) to become a focal point.

It was all simply an exciting personal project until that magazine story was published. I was blown away by the fact that readers from far afield were reacting with excitement to the style I had created — imagine my thrill to read bloggers in uber-stylish New York wanting to know where they could pick up a copy of the magazine that featured my little Aussie home.

COLLECTING, NOT HOARDING

As a stylist it's hard not to be a hoarder, but over time the eye becomes more selective and in tune with your personal style. I schedule at least one garage sale a year to filter my ever-changing collection of props and homewares. It's hard, because everything tells a story and evokes a memory of some description. A good example of this is the gorgeous vintage birdcage I doubt I shall ever let go. I used to have an obsessive collection of almost twenty; over time I've scaled that back to just this one precious cage, which more than illustrates the original appeal.

Seek out plastic sandcastle buckets of all shapes and sizes from discount and toy shops. Paint the outside with a coat of PVA wood glue and, while still wet, pour glitter over the top, making sure it gets into all the sculpted cavities. It's a messy process, best done over a lot of old newspaper. I like to use glitter in larger shards or chunks, rather than the fine variety, to achieve the best result.

IF YOU HAVE A
REAL FIREPLACE...

... cherish it; not only for its warmth in winter, but for the sturdy display shelf the mantelpiece offers. In all white, it's an ideal blank canvas inviting budding stylists to play with vignettes in varying tonal scales and forms, each whispering a different story on its decorative pedestal.

Here, glitter-covered sandcastle moulds become the unique feature piece, complemented by other finds such as glass floats with decaying rope enclosures, a reel of twine, a length of twisted driftwood, a blank paper fan, and even an antler that casts wonderful shadows across the composition.

Executed in neutrals, it is a testament to the power of texture — as opposed to colour and pattern — to create mood.

Take a closer look at this set of rustic wooden shelves and you'll notice that each shelf is cut to sit within a boarded-shut door frame. Upon each wooden plank a collection of found objects and treasured possessions creates a wonderful still-life display, all tied together by their driftwood tones; clam shells and feathers, sea-chafed rope, animal sculptures and birds' nests mingle together to tell a personal story.

Pile a day bed — an inviting spot to recline and relax — with cushions in neutral tones. Embroidered linen and flock velvet mingle here with heavier hessian and wool, each fabric lending textural and tactile interest. A simple wooden cross adorning the wall adds to the earthy scheme.

Pineapples and ferns look far from tropical here; instead, the grey-washed timber-plank dining table highlights their silvery tones, revealing a muted summery palette.

A MERMAID'S GARDEN

A free-form slab of reclaimed timber becomes a simple console table propped up on vintage trestle legs. Covered in found seaside objects, it's a pleasant greeting upon entering this home, and hints at the inspiration and aesthetic to be found further within. A group of whitewash-framed mirrors assembles on the muted grey wall, while bits of driftwood and oversized palm bark strips lean lazily in the corner.

This vignette particularly delights me as nothing within the collection seems permanently placed. With a sketchbook page ripped out and pegged to the wall, and the rosary beads casually draped over the corner of the mirror frame, it suggests nothing is too precious that it cannot be touched. In fact the tactile nature of each object invites you to pick it up, examine it, and perhaps even rearrange it to your liking.

When creating your own vignette, notice how you are analysing the scale, form and final placement of each item — it's a style laboratory waiting to be played with.

Blackened with use, an early nineteenth century fireplace adds a wintry aesthetic to this beach shack. The original brickwork in muted tones is thrown into classic relief by the clean, all-white wood panelling. Given a spray of silver paint, a weather-bleached palm frond becomes an eye-catching focal point above the simple mantelpiece, which displays an artful array of shells and seagull feathers.

A casual lounge setting is created by corner bench seating. The stone walls and whitewashed timber cladding add a sense of heritage to this space, making it feel older than perhaps it actually is. White louvres filter in the natural light and fresh air, while the decorative palm frond and large clam shell accentuate the coastal feel. Linen cushions and a lightweight throw rug create an inviting nook in which to relax and recline with a well-thumbed book, listening to the lazy ocean crashing onto the shore.

In this corner a collection of beachcombed items is piled upon a whitewashed wicker table, offering up an effortless barely-there palette. The pattern in the base of the table lamp recalls a stack of netted fishing floats, while the carved chinoiserie stool echoes the naturally sculpted form of the clam shell. A fringed throw rug adds to the sea-entangled nature of the collection.

PICKED CLEAN

An ornate but fragile chair doubles as a bedside table in this inviting setting; the rumples in the bed linen seem in textural harmony with the flaking paint on the chair's bamboo frame. With no formal bedhead, the back wall turns into a feature wall, adorned simply with hanging, mismatched glass bottles that act as vases for feathers and sprigs of vegetation.

I adore fresh flowers as the finishing touch to any interior scheme, but you'll find that introducing a vase of greenery into a beachcomber-styled room simply doesn't work. It's as if the foliage is mocking your tonal scheme, creating a jarring contradiction in line with country versus coastal.

Instead, seek out fronds and sea-battered sticks to display in simple arrangements. Hydrangeas left to dry out keep their classic shape, but day by day their colour strips out naturally to reveal a ghostly fossil of the flower that once was. Sea grasses and other native reeds are also suitable.

Or for something even further left-of-centre, seek out seabird feathers of all shapes and sizes, which can be whimsically clustered together in containers in place of the usual flower arrangements.

This distressed-look coffee table has been crafted
from a stack of wooden pallets that have been given a rough coat
of paint, the simple white highlighting the exquisite rosy hues
of the intricate shell cluster that rests on top.

Set against the patina of a peeling and once
papered-over wall, this simple dining nook evokes a nostalgic
seaside setting. Glass vessels in worn wicker and sea tones are
clustered with delicately weathered fronds. The raw-edged
muslin drapes in serene waves across the rustic dining table.

Reclaimed louvre doors are used as dramatic entryways in this home. The thoroughfare also provides an attractive spot for a hanging collection of raffia baskets. Their simple neutral tones seem to be begging for a day of exploration by the seashore.

A set of oars mounted horizontally on the wall becomes an interesting feature piece in this home. Their proportion and length perfectly suit the scale of the dining table that sits beneath. The industrial-inspired metal chairs create a setting that could be dressed in many ways.

A stack of transport pallets
becomes an inviting day bed, topped with
a selection of cushions covered in
hessian textiles. A filled-in fireplace is
painted all-white, the still-visible bricks
adding inviting texture to the space.
Canvases are stacked against the wall in
a simple display. The palm frond hanging
on the wall is pegged with photos
and postcards — a lovely idea for
displaying mementos in a novel way.

This unique bathroom was hand-constructed. Built from hay bales, the walls were rendered to produce an authentic patchy texture; rocks found on the property were inlaid into the floor and give the feeling underfoot of showering outdoors. Painted white, the bathroom instantly recalls the architecture and laid-back ambience of the Greek islands.

It's a simple but inviting space. Utilitarian exposed plumbing and piping only add to the charm. The classic Tolix stool in simple brushed aluminium nicely offsets the handmade feel of the space.

The wooden ruler nailed to the door jamb is reminiscent of flood-level markers used near low-lying waterways, here amusingly hinting that the shower may sometimes flood too.

This one-of-a-kind bathroom vanity is achieved by combining found materials that have been repurposed into a functional form. A scalloped-edge basin sets the tone and suggests the ocean as inspiration. Pebbles inlaid as a decorative border hint at beach-side holidays past. Salvaged wood in chunky forms becomes the solid foundation of the entire construction, with simple wicker baskets used as pull-out storage drawers. An oversized shell is a suitable vessel to hold a variety of loofahs and sea sponges, while the timber bathmat gives a nod to modernity. A bamboo blind filters light into the space and can be drawn for privacy.

TACTILE TEXTURES

Isn't it interesting that the most tonal of the coastal styles, when you break it down, is one of the most eclectic? This is because to make this tone-on-tone look work, you need to mix and match almost-opposites to create interest.

Rough hessian, for example, may be a perfect colour match for smooth antler bone, but placed against each other they create a tactile contrast that simply delights the senses.

Consider the number of natural textures on offer in this bathroom: the salvaged wooden beam, whitewashed timber cladding, the rocky render, chalky white overpaint, copper-toned piping, pebbly floor — as well as the additional styling elements of wicker baskets, bamboo blinds, a web-like fisherman's net and brushed aluminium seating.

It sounds like overkill, doesn't it? Yet all the elements work together to create a sense of weathered history, because they are all drawn together by their common neutral thread. The inspiration for such a scheme may well have come from something as simple as a piece of driftwood, which upon closer examination reveals a variety of intricate forms and textures, all washed over in one sea-battered hue.

This heavenly bedroom scheme is achieved through an essentially all-white palette. Layers of waffle blankets and a ruched bedcover add tactile interest, complemented by the texture of the antique shutter doors resting against the wall.

I'm not usually one for putting a bedhead against a window, but in this space the low recessed window has created the effect of a bedhead in the wall, and also provides a shelf for personal items; the window itself is like a porthole looking out to the world beyond. A lengthy strip of driftwood suggests the ocean and all its treasures are waiting nearby.

Worn whitewashed floorboards and the battered, rendered patina of the walls help create a cave-like feeling, engulfing you in a serene cocoon.

The absence of bedside tables adds to the openness and simplicity of this room. With the bedhead shelf as a storage nook, why crowd the area with more pieces?

With all the natural patinas on offer here, adding further texture in the form of furniture seems unnecessary. Sometimes you can just let a stunning piece of architecture do all the talking, especially when the aim is to evoke the isolated beauty of a seaside shack.

A trio of whitewashed iron legs from a Singer sewing machine table support a thick round of timber, creating a makeshift side table — a simple resting spot for a vase of succulents and a shell, creating another visual link to the nearby sea.

IN MEMORY OF THE SEA

This hallway still life is a dream example of using a thoroughfare to create delightful visual stories within your home. Instead of being a space you simply pass through, it invites you to stop and enjoy the tale it has to tell through its collection of found and vintage items grouped together.

An oversized hand-blown glass bottle, reminiscent of a netted nautical glass float, accents the sea-green tones of the weathered French door. The bottle holds a unique driftwood, palm frond and antler arrangement, which follows the wonderful architectural lines of the exposed staircase beam and whitewashed timber panelling on the wall behind it.

Upon the tabletop the rusty lantern and a modern table lamp, in the shape of a sea urchin, paint a portrait of life by the sea.

This setting seems to resemble a shrine to the sea.
The decorative ship's steering wheel is draped in vintage rosary beads and worn fringing, as if strewn with seaweed and barnacles. The masculine iconography of the ship's wheel contrasts with the whimsical filigree of the French candelabras; a hessian sack is used as a tactile window covering, adding to the rustic effect of the whitewashed cabinetry and rough stone walls.

To the right, an architectural piece, surely from a church, is inlaid into the wall, creating a picture-perfect shelf for a crucifix covered in shell and coral. The roughly textured walls and soft natural lighting add to the monastic feel of the space, echoed in the grey tones of the pottery vessels on the table.

Here, an eclectic mix of textures and tones is unified by the rustic neutral palette each item adheres to.

A fisherman's creel doubles as a functional storage box, hung off a door handle.

In this monochromatic corner, the combined textures and tones intermingle with each other to impressive effect. A worn grey stepladder is an ideal decorative plinth for a spiky lamp that resembles a sea urchin.

A stump of wood is painted half white to mimic a nautical pylon. It doubles as a unique side table upon which a lamp base wound with rope adds unexpected texture, echoed in the raffia-edged circular cushion that instantly suggests carefree summer afternoons. An impressive set of antlers mimics the organic shape of the reclined chair.

CAST AWAY CARES

Against an impressive pair of boatshed doors,
a hammock is strung up invitingly. The feminine embroidered
fabric is in elegant contrast to the scale and bulk of the
industrial-style entryway. A pile of cushions and a textured
throw rug provide further layers of comfort, like a suspended day
bed. A rusted anchor hanging from a rope visually counter-
balances the hammock.

A thrift shop painting depicting a panoramic waterscape of a fishing village is a window to the world beyond. The interior cladding of a boatshed is painted all-white to breathe fresh life into the place. Décor and furniture in natural materials such as bamboo add an earthy element and warm the space, while a hessian sack stamped 'Swiss Water' in an appealing watery blue complements the scheme. Bunting constructed from raw plywood drapes effortlessly, mixed in with rope and nautical hardware.

Steal away to a cabin by the sea, wide enough to fit only a bed for two. A small window gives a glimpse to the ocean beyond. It's a tranquil setting executed in neutral tones. The rope-wound lamp base and the delicate shell mobile create simple but appealing focal points. A stamped hessian sack repurposed as a cushion cover adds further texture.

A nautical-striped futon mattress
is rolled out onto the floor of this boatshed as
a make-do campsite for the night, with piles of
waffle blankets at the ready for extra warmth.
An aged lantern awaits the darkness ahead.
The fireplace inner in crackled white has an
appealing aesthetic that suits this barely-
there scheme.

This tripod stool has a wonderfully aged leather seat with detailed stitching. It sits lonesome but proud, like a fisherman's seat at the shore's edge. The feather pattern in the wallpaper reminds me of walking along a beach carpeted in an array of discarded seagull plumes.

A battered oar operates as a make-shift bolt on this set of doors, threaded through the door handles. When I found this oar, the vintage dealer shared with me how much she loved its texture; it was covered in barnacles from the bottom of the sea, but as though someone had fished it out and simply painted over the top of it for its next lease of life.

A pair of bamboo chairs offer an invitation to sit and rest awhile. Hung low, a delicate chandelier of shells adds an air of elegance. An eye-catching boat registration plate leaning casually against the boatshed wall adds an element of graphic interest.

A FEAST OF FINDS

I love an event and, for me, a table setting can be the ultimate test-lab for interior design. At your next dinner party, try out new colour schemes and collections you wouldn't normally apply to your whole home, and gauge your guests' reaction to your unexpected combinations or ideas.

Upon the paint-chipped table, a length of linen and netting is used as a table runner, setting the tone and texture. A set of mismatched painted chairs adds instant individuality; mismatched crockery in off-white is set out for each guest, as well as a linen napkin stencilled with an individual number, recalling the codes stamped onto the sea-worn decks of boats moored at fishermen's docks.

A circular section cut from a log becomes a platter on which to arrange some sailors' ale bottles, which look as if they were cast to the bottom of the ocean long ago. The ivory candles dripping in wax heighten the mood as evening falls.

It feels as if everything has been collected from a walk along the sand dunes earlier in the day, and reimagined into the table setting for that evening.

A mound of wicker fishing creels
creates a starting point for the
beachcomber palette. In muted neutrals,
the thatched weaving mixes a variety of
worn textures, one against the other.
Apply the same successful contrast in
your decorating solutions by opting for
tactile textiles and homewares that mingle
interestingly, even in all-nude hues.

A sofa is given a unique look by being re-upholstered in a soft hessian, setting the texture and palette for this living room; for comfort, avoid the hard, itchy variety of this cloth! On the floor a patchwork rug in similar tones adds interest. A simple white crate is turned on its side as a small coffee table, upon which an enamel bowl displays the latest beachside finds. To complement the lounge upholstery, a post-office sack finds new life as a square cushion cover, and a knotted combination of lace and net becomes a tactile throw. A large wicker pendant shade, hung low, is given a single stripe of white paint to add a nautical air.

MORE BEACHCOMBER
STYLING IDEAS

➤➤ Ropes almost threadbare from the nautical adventures they've endured can be put to good use. Create a dividing wall with vertical drops of rope, separating a space delightfully while letting light and air through. A similar effect could take the place of a staircase's banister and rungs.

➤➤ Fishing traps and gadgets can also take on new forms. Hang fishing nets and lobster pots around a single light bulb dropped from the ceiling; the intertwined lattice will cast a unique shadow play onto your walls at night.

➤➤ Distressed doors that serve no functional purpose can be rested against a wall to add layers of interest.

➤➤ Upcycle wooden transport pallets or cable reels into all manner of furniture: pile them up as bed bases or coffee tables. Their exposure to the elements leaves the wood with a ghostly patina similar to sunbleached driftwood.

➤➤ Suspend a bare driftwood branch as a rail for hanging pots and plants, or collect smaller bits of driftwood and apply them en masse to transform a piece with coastal flair. For example, use them to cover a circular mirror frame in an outward 'sunburst' motif, or craft them into a circular door wreath.

➤➤ Find an unexpected use for natural materials. Rustic flooring can be used as a wall cladding, adding visual impact to feature walls, or as bedheads. Even inexpensive bamboo screens from a hardware store can be used as a make-do bedhead, exuding a natural texture synonymous with the beachcomber look.

➤➤ For design impact, group like items: a collection of rough-edged raffia sunhats perched on hooks becomes a striking and cost-effective design feature that captures memories of relaxed coastal walks, no matter how far your house is from the shore.

Chapter 2

Seafarer

A MOODY PALETTE INSPIRED BY THE AGE OF EXPLORATION AND THE WATERY TONES OF THE OCEAN

THE REAL VOYAGE OF DISCOVERY
CONSISTS NOT IN SEEKING NEW LANDSCAPES,
BUT IN HAVING NEW EYES.

– MARCEL PROUST

A world of exploration

➤ **There is a world out there waiting to be explored.**

Every pioneer – explorer, sailor or pirate – carried tools of their trade. Today, we can uncover these tools at antique stores and archives, appreciating them less for their function and more for their worn beauty and history. If only a dog-eared leather compass case could tell of many voyages navigated across distant seas...

Take your cue for this scheme from a vintage treasure chest of tools and fishing tackle that might have once belonged to a daring explorer or sea-weathered fisherman.

DARK AND STORMY

WAVES SEEM TO HAVE WASHED OVER EVERY ITEM ON THIS MOOD BOARD. Vintage paintings of violent seascapes create the palette itself, a mix of austere greys and deep midnight blues. Masculine metals, such as battered pewter, suit the muted mix of tones. Detailed, crosshatched illustrations of sailing ships are replicated on fabric and ceramics. Grotesque monsters of the deep oceans provide dramatic iconography. An oyster shell and pale feather seem fitting here too, balancing the harder features.

Seafarer
(noun)

A TRAVELLER WHO GOES BY SEA.
A LESS COMMON TERM
FOR SAILOR.

SEAFARER
COLOUR PALETTE

A deep aquatic palette emerges from the depths of a midnight ocean. The inky blue (6), almost squid-ink black (7), and stormy ocean greys (3, 4) suggest the ripples on the water's surface. Notice how the ocean changes depending on the time of day and season of the year, from angry navy to crystal clear azure (5). Elements of dirty oyster (2) and white (1) provide contrast and keep the palette crisp.

The dark and stormy colour palette is re-created here in paint pigments that have been poured into individual vintage vials like messages in bottles.

SEEK OUT THESE ELEMENTS TO CREATE A SEAFARING ATMOSPHERE IN YOUR HOME.

➤ Industrial enamel light shades ➤ Old lanterns ➤ Vintage manuals on sailing and the sea (for their illustrations as much as their words) ➤ Anything 'anchor' ➤ Original maritime signal flags ➤ Rope ➤ Sailing boat toys and models (cluster together a collection) ➤ Thrift-store and paint-by-numbers artworks of stormy seas ➤ Vintage globes, atlases, maps and wall charts ➤ Ships in bottles ➤ Messages in bottles ➤ Woven bottles and flagons ➤ Paper boats ➤ Fishermen's baskets, creels and tackle boxes ➤ Vintage luggage and suitcases ➤ Sea chests and shipping cases ➤ Barrels and half-barrels ➤ Caged lightbulb enclosures ➤ Fishing nets, reels and rods ➤ Pirate flags ➤ Fish-shaped plates and platters ➤ Barnacle-covered treasures ➤ Trophies and tarnished vessels ➤ Pewter mugs and jugs

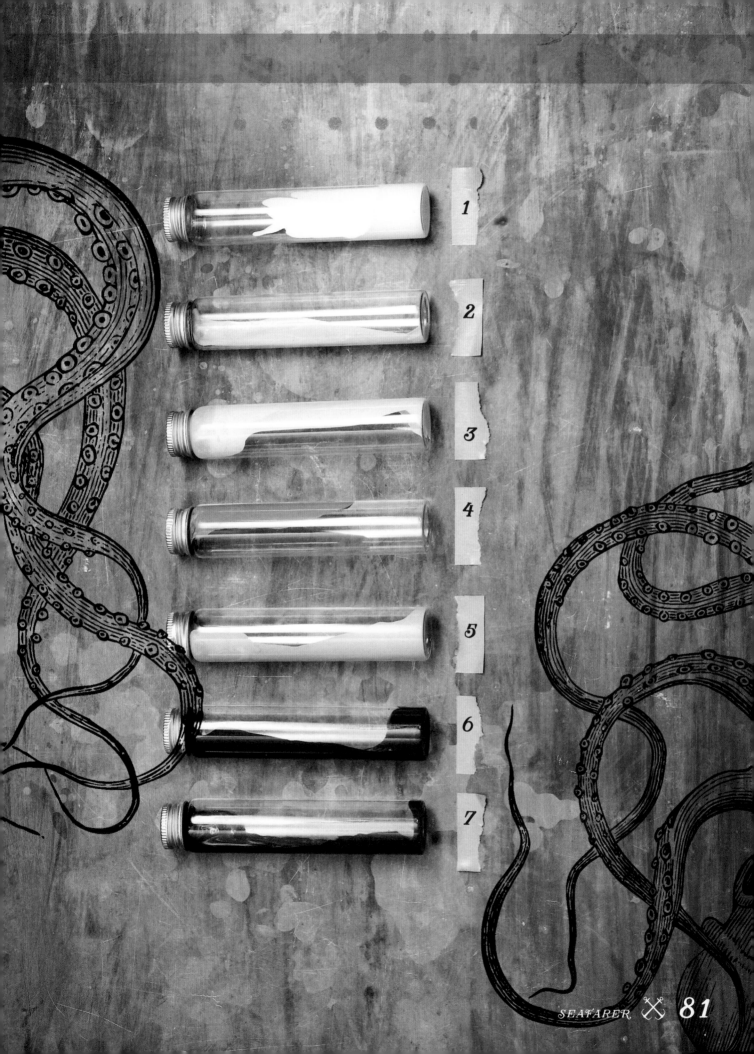

MAN AGAINST THE SEA

I THOUGHT I WOULD SAIL ABOUT A LITTLE AND SEE THE WATERY PART OF THE WORLD. WHENEVER I FIND MYSELF GROWING GRIM ABOUT THE MOUTH; WHENEVER IT IS A DAMP, DRIZZLY NOVEMBER IN MY SOUL... THEN, I ACCOUNT IT HIGH TIME TO GET TO SEA AS SOON AS I CAN. THERE IS MAGIC IN IT. YES, AS EVERY ONE KNOWS, MEDITATION AND WATER ARE WEDDED FOR EVER.

WHY UPON YOUR FIRST VOYAGE AS A PASSENGER, DID YOU YOURSELF FEEL SUCH A MYSTICAL VIBRATION, WHEN FIRST TOLD THAT YOU AND YOUR SHIP WERE NOW OUT OF SIGHT OF LAND? WHY DID THE OLD PERSIANS HOLD THE SEA HOLY? WHY DID THE GREEKS GIVE IT A SEPARATE DEITY, AND OWN BROTHER OF JOVE? SURELY ALL THIS IS NOT WITHOUT MEANING.

—*Moby Dick*, by Herman Melville, 1851

It seems mankind has always been fascinated by the sea: the scale of it; the unpredictability of it. This love-hate relationship with our greatest natural wonder has been much explored in both literature and film.

A plethora of titles tackle the tension between mankind and the sea. But one aspect is constant: a recurring, universal and timeless theme of man made small against its wonder. A plotline that continually emerges is one in which man (and it usually is a man rather than a woman) is left to battle out his individual psychological drama against the wide open space of the ocean. There's no other place where, as the introduction to *Moby Dick* suggests, such a mirror is held up to our inner selves. Perhaps this is why so many of us long for an ocean escape, to sit by the water for even a moment, to gather our thoughts in the fresh sea air.

I love how natural light flickers over this slightly ghostly setting. This corner desk and chair capture the dark and stormy palette wonderfully. There's a sense of history and heritage to the pieces, but they're not too precious and are all a bit rough around the edges.

The table is worn and scratched from use; only fragments of its original black lacquer survive. The upholstered chair is splitting at the seams, revealing startling flashes of red upholstery lining that add an accent colour to the overall scheme. Worn black rope instantly places the scenario in a seafaring context. The table lamp has a simple industrial presence.

Piles of pen and ink tattoo sketches and vintage books add texture and interest. Pick up a set of ink nibs at your local art store and rediscover the simple drawing process. Or perhaps sharpen the end of a feather to make a quill for coloured ink — get the creativity soaring.

I have been inked — tastefully, of course! I've chosen tattoos based on subjects I consider important to me and hope I shall never regret them, in design or placement.

Many tattoo motifs in today's popular culture have their design roots in maritime subculture. These have often become signature designs, in deep black outlines with splashes of navy blue and red ink to complete the nautical palette.

Mythical mermaids, navigational constellations, sailing galleons, scaly fish, fantastical sea creatures and pin-up girls are common sailor fare. Early on, seamen used this graphic language on their body as a visual bond of brotherhood. Designs might record their adventures at sea, places they'd visited or their on-board rank.

Iconography was also used to protect against maritime superstitions. Sailors traditionally inked religious symbols on their bodies in the belief that these tattoos would ward off violent storms at sea caused by their particular wrathful god.

My next ink pick would be a traditional anchor. The iconography speaks volumes; forged of cold, hard, heavy steel, the anchor is also the reliable hardware used to connect us to the land we choose to call home. And isn't that what we're all looking for, seafarer or not?

Opt for a wrought iron bed, a classic design that
will never date. There are some great reproduction versions
on the market now in pop colours and shiny metallics. If
you're lucky enough to find an original, chances are the
bedhead will be intact but the wire base long gone. If so, use
timber battens to remake the base as a slat bed and
strengthen the overall frame. Depending on the condition of
the frame, you might leave the enamel coating flaking off in
parts, but if it's running to rust, seek out a professional to
scrape back the tube to raw material and respray it.

A stack of vintage suitcases makes a unique bedside
table, while also providing ample storage for spare bed linen.

The colour palette in this room is a serene scheme of soft
greys, barely-there neutrals and washed-out blues.

Mix and match different bed linen to interesting effect.
Here, felt army blankets with a contrasting stripe are thrown
over an embroidered bedcover and mismatched sheeting. But
the interesting choice is the vintage linen sack, repurposed
(and stuffed with two, side-by-side, duck-feather pillows) to
become a lengthy statement bolster.

Blue ticking fabric stretched over the mattress is a
classic option. Seek out this stripe in linens and soft fabrics
wherever you can, so that you always have a stash handy.

If you can't have ocean views, find a panoramic image of
the sea and hang it low over your bedhead, like a porthole to
an imaginary horizon. The artwork here was an op shop find,
bought for a few dollars, and its ageing yellow tarnish adds
to the sense of history in the room's scheme.

A zinc-caged lamp introduces a lovely metallic sheen to
the room without looking showy. Hung low at the bedside, it
adds to the atmosphere of sailors' sleeping quarters in some
great ship. Just one lamp is fine — adding a second pendant
to the other side of the bed would look far too matchy-
matchy in this understated scheme.

HMSO   MANUAL OF SEAMANSHIP

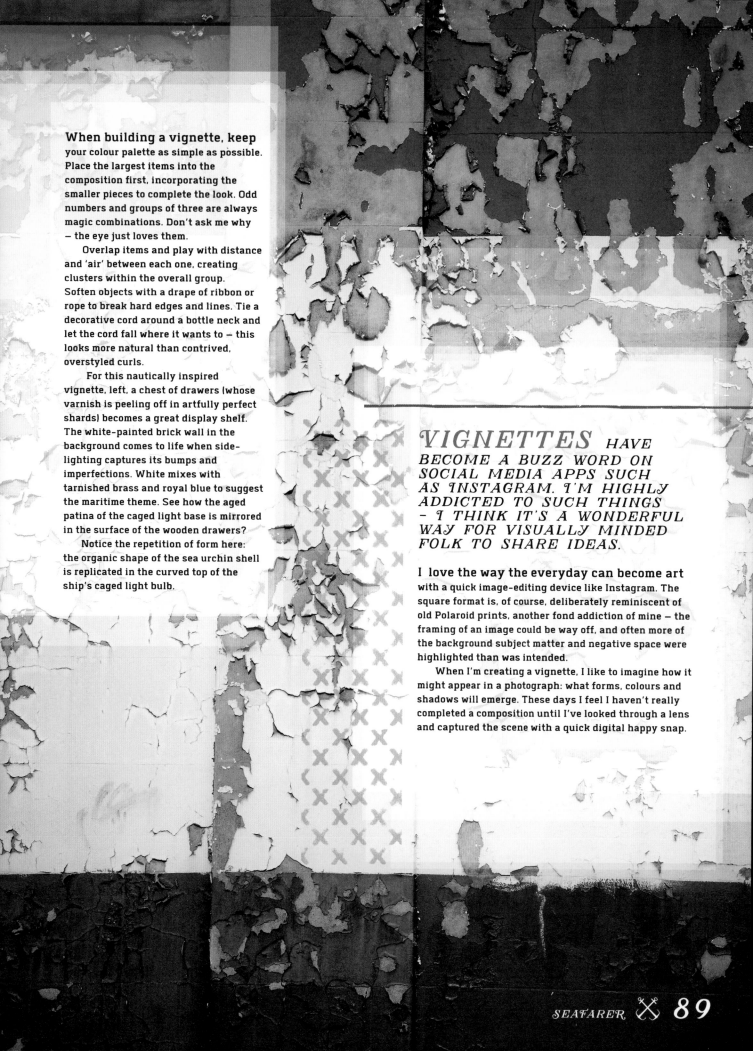

When building a vignette, keep your colour palette as simple as possible. Place the largest items into the composition first, incorporating the smaller pieces to complete the look. Odd numbers and groups of three are always magic combinations. Don't ask me why – the eye just loves them.

Overlap items and play with distance and 'air' between each one, creating clusters within the overall group. Soften objects with a drape of ribbon or rope to break hard edges and lines. Tie a decorative cord around a bottle neck and let the cord fall where it wants to – this looks more natural than contrived, overstyled curls.

For this nautically inspired vignette, left, a chest of drawers (whose varnish is peeling off in artfully perfect shards) becomes a great display shelf. The white-painted brick wall in the background comes to life when side-lighting captures its bumps and imperfections. White mixes with tarnished brass and royal blue to suggest the maritime theme. See how the aged patina of the caged light base is mirrored in the surface of the wooden drawers?

Notice the repetition of form here: the organic shape of the sea urchin shell is replicated in the curved top of the ship's caged light bulb.

VIGNETTES HAVE BECOME A BUZZ WORD ON SOCIAL MEDIA APPS SUCH AS INSTAGRAM. I'M HIGHLY ADDICTED TO SUCH THINGS – I THINK IT'S A WONDERFUL WAY FOR VISUALLY MINDED FOLK TO SHARE IDEAS.

I love the way the everyday can become art with a quick image-editing device like Instagram. The square format is, of course, deliberately reminiscent of old Polaroid prints, another fond addiction of mine – the framing of an image could be way off, and often more of the background subject matter and negative space were highlighted than was intended.

When I'm creating a vignette, I like to imagine how it might appear in a photograph: what forms, colours and shadows will emerge. These days I feel I haven't really completed a composition until I've looked through a lens and captured the scene with a quick digital happy snap.

The most magical inclusion in this room for me
is the grey fishing net resting over the bedhead. Its placement
suggests a maritime-style dreamcatcher. An original caged light
bulb hung low by the bedside is a statement piece, casting
wonderful shadows over the space. Notice the wooden crate as a
bedside table — the perfect height when placed on its side.
Unintentionally, it has a sea reference with 'Seal Co' stamped on
one surface (sometimes these objects seem to gravitate together
to create delightful coincidences).

On the bedside table an original ship's bell doubles as an
alarm clock and vintage books tell classic tales of the sea.

The overall palette is serene, but individual elements are
working hard: the scheme is balanced by tiny details such as the
muted blue stripe on the bed cover that matches the vintage
book spine. Hospital-style blankets give a utilitarian simplicity
to the bed while adding comfort and warmth with their layers of
waffled texture.

Horizontal wood panelling

instantly says 'boathouse' in this bathroom. It's a brave choice: abandoning functional tiles for painted timber surfaces to create a homely cocoon for bathing.

Here, too, is a good example of grouping like objects to exaggerate their effect: bevelled-edged vintage mirrors each have their own individualistic shapes, but also come together as a like-minded visual family.

A row of black wrought-iron wall hooks are functional but you can add whimsy: the knotted fishing net hung from them drapes onto the floor and also introduces an element of natural texture and colour, breaking up the room's otherwise monochromatic scheme. Natural sea sponges are functional but also provide lovely organic forms.

Opt for a claw-foot bathtub for ultimate luxury. In this room it's set centre stage, away from all four walls, which gives an overall sense of space and lightness around what is essentially a large and clunky item.

Roll out a striped rug to add a maritime flavour to any space. The deep indigo stripe in this design is almost the colour of squid ink and adds a subtle variation in the overall scheme.

A worn leather tool trunk is stencil-sprayed with a skull and crossbones for a hint of piratical humour.

Nautical iconography is hand-carved into square, ink-stained wood panels that are hung in a simple threesome on the white wall. Notice how practical illustrations of sailing knots have become their own unique art form. Seek out these original diagrams in books and manuals.

The chair seat is reupholstered in a plain neutral linen. Arranged on the chair is a simple vignette of old books and a fisherman's reel, with a primitive-looking handmade lure guaranteed to attract any passing fish!

Create the atmosphere of a
sailors' mess for your next dinner party.
Tolix chairs — real or replica — in raw
aluminium create an instant utilitarian
vibe. They appear to be more function
than comfort, yet, surprisingly, offer both.

Black, a colour I am rarely drawn to, is
the featured hue here, inspired by the
pirate flag. The look is far from heavy
because it's balanced by the neutrals of
the rug's stripe and the antique pine table.
The table's turned legs might be
traditional but the overall look is kept
modern by the eclectic styling. The
mismatched crockery setting features sea
iconography. Fish platters appear to float
on a grey, frayed muslin fabric scrap used
as an impromptu table runner.

Oversized glossy black enamel
industrial shades are mock-hung in a rope
and pulley system, anchored to one table
leg to create a fun effect at the diners'
eye level.

Despite the black shades, only the
overhead skylight illuminates this dining
space, so the huge, dark-framed mirror
resting against the wall is a great way to
bounce light around the room.

YO HO HO AND A BOTTLE OF RUM...

Hunt down wicker flagons and cork-topped bottles at markets and garage sales
and gather them into a pirate-inspired collection.

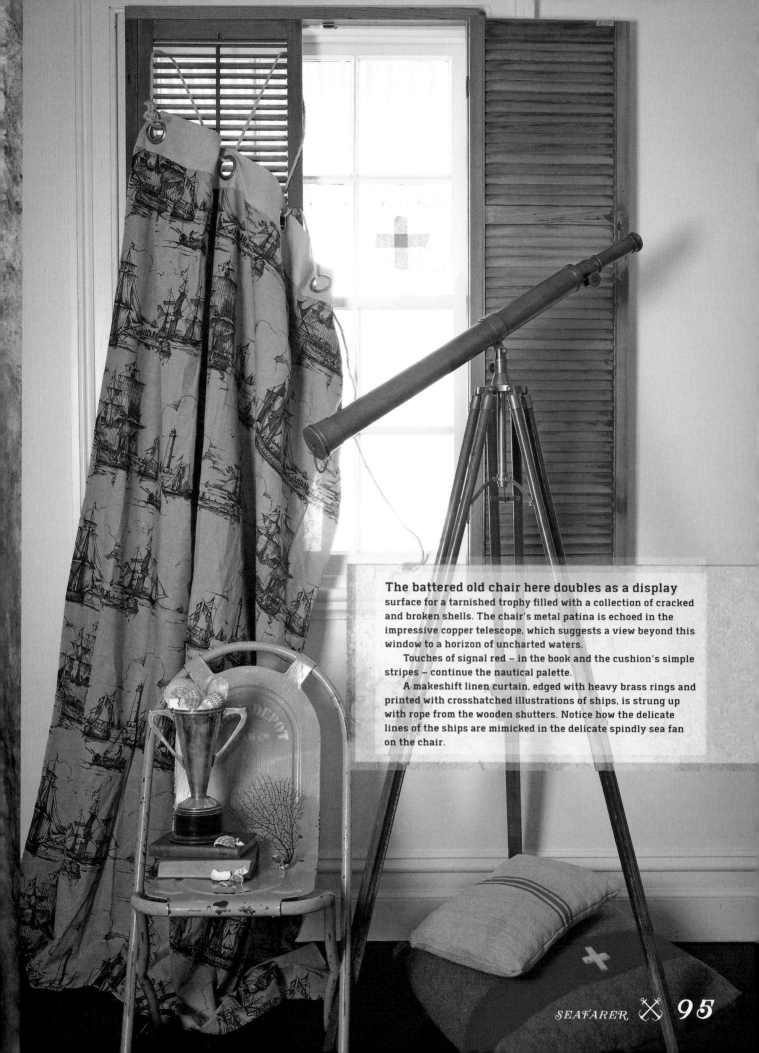

The battered old chair here doubles as a display surface for a tarnished trophy filled with a collection of cracked and broken shells. The chair's metal patina is echoed in the impressive copper telescope, which suggests a view beyond this window to a horizon of uncharted waters.

Touches of signal red – in the book and the cushion's simple stripes – continue the nautical palette.

A makeshift linen curtain, edged with heavy brass rings and printed with crosshatched illustrations of ships, is strung up with rope from the wooden shutters. Notice how the delicate lines of the ships are mimicked in the delicate spindly sea fan on the chair.

This bathroom receives a theatrical underwater makeover with the addition of an octopus-covered shower curtain. The illustrated imagery of the sea creature seems fitting with the splash and spray that occur in a bathtub shower. It creates a delightful drama.

Abandon the usual plastic circular clasps and use rope instead to string up the fanciful design. An oversized rope tassel becomes the ultimate 'soap on a rope', draped over the side of the gorgeous claw-foot bathtub.

Oh, the tales this steamer trunk could tell... A classic sailor's blue-and-white striped tunic is draped with a rough-edged linen scarf and herringbone vintage tuxedo vest, decorated with a royal blue and gold medal. A rolled-up treasure map and a battered lantern create an atmosphere of adventure.

I adore the textures of this vintage travelling box with its drawers, compartments and built-in hanging space. What a wonderful way to travel and treasure your possessions — and what a shame they don't make luggage like this anymore.

A trunk like this could be used as a wardrobe in a small space such as a studio apartment, or set up in a corner as a storage and display home for your favourite pieces. It has plenty of hanging room and compartments for showing off all types of treasures, not just clothes.

An impressive library of vintage books runs floor to ceiling around this space, creating the atmosphere of a marine biologist's study. Glass domes hold, frame and magnify unique shells and clusters of barnacles.

The circular rug is hand-patched from remnants of drop sheets, creating a unique map of the world. Each visible stitch on its surface works as part of the overall design, and the pencil tracings of continents and islands are still apparent.

Flags and stencilled sacks are re-used as cushion covers – the Union Jack adds not only a richness to the colour palette but a sense of history and heritage. And the stud detailing on the black upholstered chairs adds a hint of sexiness that prevents the room becoming stuffy.

In this home most windows have been dressed with interior wooden shutters, each one slightly different, cut from larger doors to suit their new use. This option is both cost effective and more interesting than freshly fitted plantation shutters.

The grand scale of this pale stone fireplace makes an impressive background for the dark and stormy setting. The neutral tones of the limestone set the base palette. A hefty fisherman's net is strung up across the mantle, its folds softening the starkness of the empty grate. It falls naturally into a wave and on this temporary visual sea sits an intricately detailed, cast-iron model ship.

A comfortable but cracked leather armchair has been given an update – its seat wrapped in a pirate flag. The colour balances the black introduced by the model ship and void of the fireplace. Heavy worn blankets are spread over the floor as a rug and draped over the armchair for extra warmth. This is the ideal spot to sit down after dinner and enjoy a glass of seafarer's port from a wicker flagon.

This styled scenario demonstrates an interesting use of scale, proportion and fun – all essential aspects in creating a unique visual solution.

When using the ocean as inspiration for an interior scheme, consider how the theatricality of this natural element can be reinterpreted, along with suitably scaled man-made imagery.

The chunky fishing net draped to resemble the sea has a wonderful playfulness. I took the idea from my first stage design – Edward Bond's *The Sea*, which was part of my graduation from a set and costume design degree at NIDA.

The play is yet another tale of man fighting and struggling against the ocean, almost drowning before he washes up on shore. Our solution to the logistical task of staging a storm at sea was quite elegant: a lengthy curved curtain bar mimicking the organic motion of the ocean ran the width of the entire stage, beginning at floor level. As the stage lights went up, the music grew in volume, wind and rain sound effects created a multi-sensory experience and the curtain rose to reveal metre upon metre of hand-pleated organza billowing over the stage. The actors and man-made elements of furniture and props were dwarfed by the seascape that hung as the constant backdrop. I have tried a similar approach in this room.

Experiment with dramatic use of proportion in your next interior solution. Choose outdoor objects such as oars and nets to create a visual contrast to the norm and add an element of the unexpected. Introducing this dash of playfulness will soften any overall difference in the scale of the room's elements.

GOTHIC TREASURES AND EMPTY FRAMES

This corner has a wonderfully unnerving feel to it. An empty freestanding mantle stands where once a fire would have smouldered. Instead of its original purpose, here the mantle becomes the frame for a decorative still life of stacked vintage suitcases, each hand-painted with the owner's monogram. The wooden boat, positioned in front of the logstack, adds a nautical air. The logs themselves suggest a winteriness that suits this cooler palette.

The chair is a favourite of mine. It sits perfectly in this scheme: peeling layers of upholstery reveal wadding and hessian; its blue ticking fabric and flashes of red lining suggest a sailor's uniform. The hefty rope wound into a sculptural statement piece on the mantle is a perfect finishing touch.

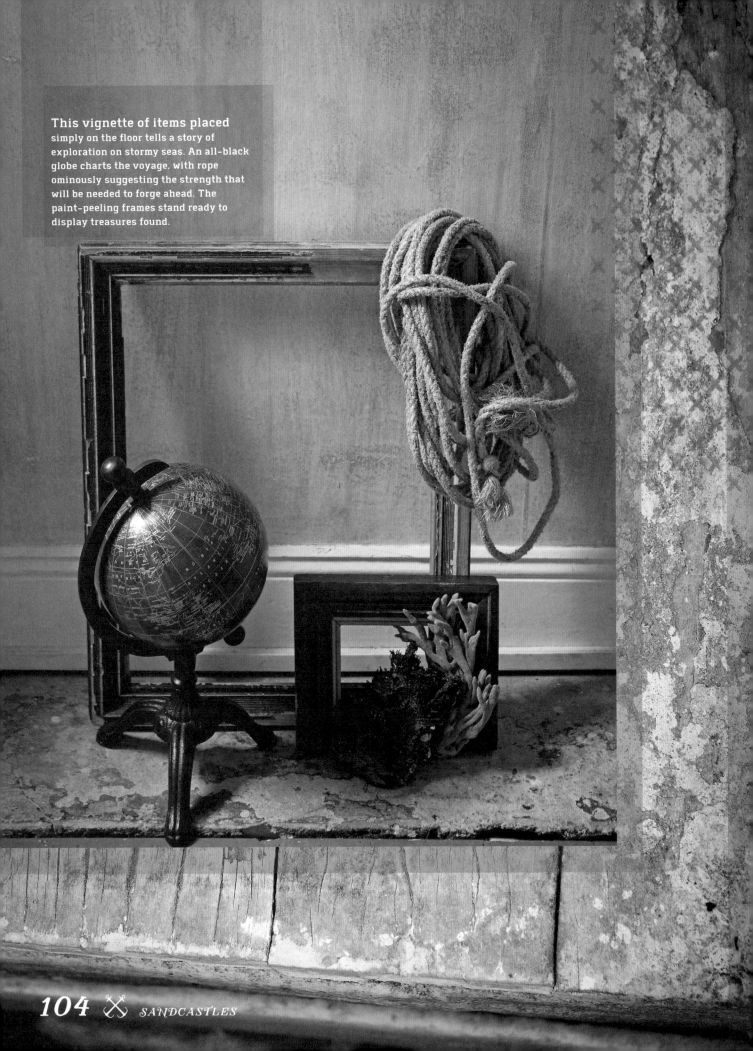

This vignette of items placed simply on the floor tells a story of exploration on stormy seas. An all-black globe charts the voyage, with rope ominously suggesting the strength that will be needed to forge ahead. The paint-peeling frames stand ready to display treasures found.

With its backdrop of peeling wallpaper and paint, this terrace house exudes a dark, gothic atmosphere. A central fireplace painted glossy black, complete with an impressive plaster ship firescreen, is the initial focal point of this room. On and above the mantle is clustered a trio of aged artworks, including a stormy seascape and partially completed cross-stitch of a skull and crossbones, fitting for the Victorian era setting. A grand piano with appealingly wonky keys and broken mechanisms is clearly for decorative rather than musical purposes. It has been draped with a sea-worn fishing net, whose pale shape also puts us in mind of the spider webs that might be expected in such a setting.

FORM AND FUNCTION

In this crumbling passageway a row of mismatched hooks
provides not only functional hanging space but also an
appealing decorative piece in its own right. The nautical story
has been continued here with a cluster of aged possessions: a
worn rope, a fisherman's creel and a felted admiral's hat.

On this ebony mantle the cluster of candlesticks and candelabras is also mismatched in shape, but linked by common pewter. Model ships have been spray-painted satin black to highlight their sails and rigging – they appear as shadowy figures against a pale horizon. A duo of dark-painted glittered sandcastles continues the gothic aesthetic.

This bathroom setting is a wonderful example of grouping like objects. The collection of shaving cabinets are all of different shape and scale but their grey patina provides a common link. An impressive aged wooden cabinet becomes a unique vanity with a modern basin fitted on top. Fresh hand towels are rolled up in an old wooden cigar box.

A timber-battened plaster
wall has been left purposely battered and
cracked, revealing the original Victorian
craftsmanship beneath. We certainly
don't build houses like this anymore...

STEP INTO THE DEN

Treasure chests become coffee tables and upturned half barrels are used for seating in this styled scenario. With the pewter mugs and coffee pot laid out, the atmosphere is that of a pirate card den. The moss green brickwork and worn grey floorboards render this a muted, dusty palette. The shutter doors are beautifully aged and rest artfully against the walls, with no real purpose other than to add a layer of texture and interest to the space. A cluster of butler's domes hangs on the wall, as in a ship's galley. The whale cushion is appealing but also practical, adding some comfort to the wooden barrel stool.

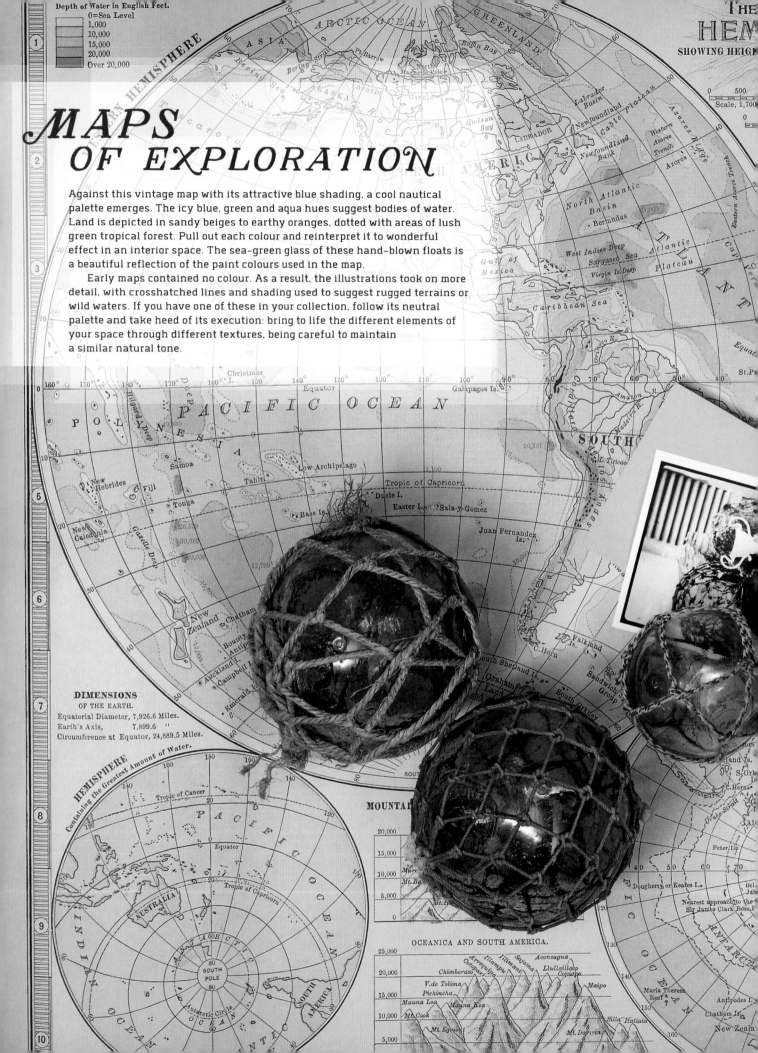

MAPS
OF EXPLORATION

Against this vintage map with its attractive blue shading, a cool nautical palette emerges. The icy blue, green and aqua hues suggest bodies of water. Land is depicted in sandy beiges to earthy oranges, dotted with areas of lush green tropical forest. Pull out each colour and reinterpret it to wonderful effect in an interior space. The sea-green glass of these hand-blown floats is a beautiful reflection of the paint colours used in the map.

Early maps contained no colour. As a result, the illustrations took on more detail, with crosshatched lines and shading used to suggest rugged terrains or wild waters. If you have one of these in your collection, follow its neutral palette and take heed of its execution: bring to life the different elements of your space through different textures, being careful to maintain a similar natural tone.

Clear sky blues, ocean sea-greens and glassy teals and turquoises all mix to wondrous effect in this dining setting. A circular theme links the clusters of globes and paper lanterns with the oversized industrial clock behind.

The pre-loved kitchen table has been instantly updated by painting the legs and frame turquoise, leaving the wooden top unpainted to reveal its age. The chairs are a collection of roadside finds; in creamy antique whites and with flaking paint edges they are linked by their classic bentwood and spindled forms. The fresh blue and white stripe of the rug lifts the overall scheme.

The buffet cabinet made from recycled boat timbers is a great find. The distressed shards of blue and aqua paint add to the vibrancy of the room without overwhelming it. A model wooden boat sits on top of the buffet as a decorative piece, draped in faded, inky-blue, dip-dyed cotton rope.

ONE IS NEVER ENOUGH

Notice how displaying these hand-blown glass fishing floats en masse magnifies their appeal and visual impact. They range in glass colour – from clear to dark navy – scale and state of disrepair. Each is knotted with rope, some almost threadbare from saltwater, and hung from the wall. These sorts of once-functional items can add individual style to your scheme.

Here, a narrow, otherwise under-used, passageway becomes a display alcove. The framed vintage map resting against the wall sets the palette for the collection: a floodwater yardstick; an oar in a pleasing shade of blue; a whitewashed lobster pot showing off its sculptural form; and a rope bag cushioning a pair of glass sea floats. The finishing touch? An industrial brass letter T – for Tim, of course (always make your collections personal and relevant to you).

This bathroom glistens with classic subway tiles, in frosted green rather than their usual white. The feature, however, is the shower curtain made from a sail, stamped with its United States Navy number and hung from nautical-style hooks. The lovely opaque fabric of the sailcloth filters the natural light from the window.

The appealing colours of the
vintage map are expanded into a full room
palette here. The aquamarine shutter door
instantly creates a fresh tone for the
furnishings to follow. The pure-white
ceramic stool used as a side table and the
oyster-grey wicker chair make a laid-back
ensemble. It suits that the bathroom
beyond the shutter is tiled in aqua
mosaics. Natural forms emerge in the
shell-framed artisan mirror and the white
coral sculptural focal piece. Vintage atlas
pages make a unique floor cover – they
can be permanently lacquered to
floorboards with a clear protective
coating. The map theme is picked up in
the wicker chair cushion and notice the
faded blue cotton rope coiled on top of the
ceramic stool as a mat for the coral.

⚓ SANDCASTLES

A sky-blue flaking shutter door
is the colour inspiration for this scheme
– it is perfectly offset by the white walls
to instantly suggest a Mediterranean
palette. The clear blue is balanced by the
green-tinged glass of the floats, while the
white porcelain trophy adds crispness to
the scheme. Natural texture is provided by
the oversized clam shell and the table legs
crafted as a bundle of driftwood. An
industrial hook is mounted into the space
as if it had always been there – the cotton
rope hung from it softens the look. The
rattan sofa mimics the texture of the
plaited rope and a fringed throw, with a
simple nautical stripe border, becomes a
neat floor covering.

SIGNALS,
SIGNS & SYMBOLS

Nautical flags and symbols communicated important messages, and their block colour-coded system also creates a classic palette to draw from. A vintage Union Jack is the starting point for this scheme: faded royal blue mixes with a once-striking red against the ageing calico. The signal flags continue the colour palette and add more geometric patterns, while their manuals add a deeper level of meaning and interest. Plaited red, white and blue thread is another visual reminder of the colour bond (and reminiscent of the borders of airmail envelopes). A schoolboy's tie is a nice example of the formality of the same colour combination.

The orginal paint scheme of this historic maritime building provided the palette here. The lower portion of the half-tone wall is a muted ocean blue – the ideal backdrop for a pair of turquoise wicker chairs. Their traditional shape suggests history but they have been instantly updated by the fresh paint colour. The thin red band running around the wall at mid-height is mirrored on the striped rug, stools and mounted buoys that have become statement design pieces. The simple replica Tolix stool used as a side table adds an air of industry that reminds us of the building's past. The old stone fireplace balances the cement tones of the windowsill and is kept plain and unadorned, letting the inspiring architecture speak for itself.

In this maritime barracks the wooden hooks are the perfect hanging place for a string of signal flags. An old school chart illustrating the dissection of a cod fish was a great find – it is strung up against the window to create a temporary blind.

A set of flaking doors creates an intriguing entrance to this space, left, adding a darker grey into the already dark and stormy palette. Pin-up girls are tacked on the door, suggesting sailors' quarters, the splashes of colour complementing the seat cushion, which is covered with a vintage signal flag. The graphic interest of such styling has enormous effect on this space. The bold red cross of the cushion is in turn balanced by the oar mounted on the wall. A felt blanket in deep grey, with nautical striped edge detailing, adds a layer of comfort to the cool-coloured setting.

This wallpaper, right, reminds me of Japanese watercolour paintings of koi carp and makes this a truly impressive space. This is a small room, with little natural light, so what could have become a drab, dark corner has instead been brought to life by wrapping the space in this print. Each fish has a slight metallic sheen, reminiscent of scales, against the serene ocean blue background. To ground the wallpaper's glossiness, the floor has been covered with hessian sacks sewn together to form a natural carpet. The sacks are stamped with red and blue icons and shipping text and instantly add a nautical feel. A heavy chair is used as a weight from which to tie a pair of massive red wicker lanterns. Although they have an elongated shape, they instantly set me in mind of wooden lobster pots. A worn net resting against one wall completes the setting.

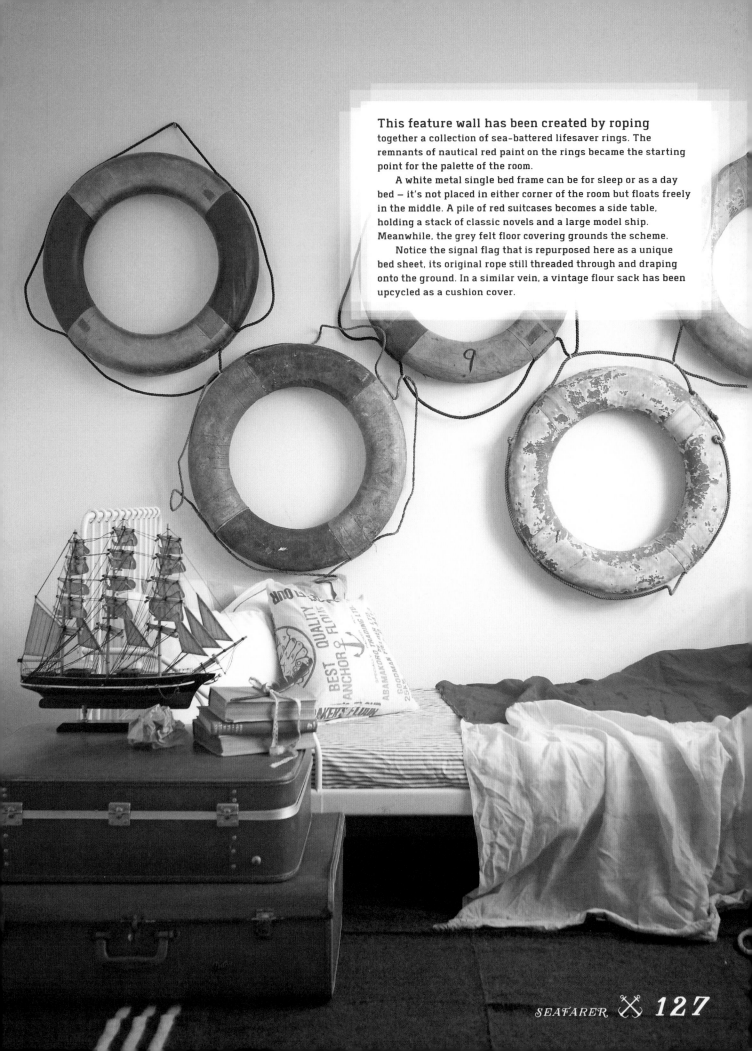

This feature wall has been created by roping together a collection of sea-battered lifesaver rings. The remnants of nautical red paint on the rings became the starting point for the palette of the room.

A white metal single bed frame can be for sleep or as a day bed – it's not placed in either corner of the room but floats freely in the middle. A pile of red suitcases becomes a side table, holding a stack of classic novels and a large model ship. Meanwhile, the grey felt floor covering grounds the scheme.

Notice the signal flag that is repurposed here as a unique bed sheet, its original rope still threaded through and draping onto the ground. In a similar vein, a vintage flour sack has been upcycled as a cushion cover.

This is one of my favourite shacks at Melbourne's iconic Brighton Beach. The paint colours are simple, but the focal point is the row of hand-painted signal flags above its door.

LAYERS OF INTEREST

In this quaint shack every surface is covered with vintage fishing paraphernalia. Given the small scale of the room, you might think this volume of decorative pieces would be cluttering. However, I find it adds layers of interest; a visual history that connects the home to its setting next to a fishing jetty.

The red and white stripes of the lighthouses are echoed in the chair fabric and layers of small rugs and on a vintage fold-out fishing stool used as a side table.

The classic red, white and blue nautical palette is enlivened with a dash of yellow. The colours are all somewhat muted to add to the vintage feel.

Decorative lighthouses are not often my go-to pieces for interior design, but in this room they are clustered in various shapes and sizes to heighten their appeal. Look closely and you'll see they all date from different eras, which adds to the interest of the display.

This fishing-related collection makes a delightful display at the entrance to this fishing lodge. The circular nets mirror the shape of the quoits set, which in turn mirrors the appearance of sea-worn rope. Dots of red are picked up in the antique fish lures and striped wooden lighthouse.

Maritime signal flags speak an international
visual language: single flags represent individual letters of the alphabet, or can be combined for universal meanings. Here they have been sewn into cushion covers and their colours mingle together appealingly.

This room was built around a huge vintage boat model. The architect designed an alcove that, by day, is side-lit by thin panels of glass louvres, while, at night, halogen downlights create different shadows on the ropes and masts. The classic form of the bamboo sofa with its curved armrests brings another era and style into the nautical setting.

This kitchen, while modern,
simple and very functional, also has a
nautical and industrial air. The checked
red-and-white splashback is a simple
effect evoking nautical precision. The two
industrial-look swivel stools turn the
island bench into an informal dining area,
lit by a classic utilitarian pendant shade.
With this style of kitchen, opt for classic
hardware such as simple wooden pantry
knobs and the porcelain basin with pulley
handle taps. The lightly sanded edge of
the wooden bench breaks up the overall
pristine look. The decorative wicker
flagons suggest a ship's galley kitchen.

MORE SEAFARER *STYLING IDEAS*

➤➤ Get swept away in seafarer style by using large-format maps and charts as wall hangings, or tear up a whole atlas and decoupage the pages as unique wallpaper.

➤➤ Pile well-travelled luggage, such as sea chests and steamer trunks, to table height to magnify their effect and give them new purpose.

➤➤ Revamp an old suitcase or leather doctor's bag with a nautical-inspired stencil: skull and crossbones or anchor graphics suit the look.

➤➤ Metal and enamel industrial lighting suggest a bygone era, when items were built to last. Their hard-edged forms would be at home in a harbourside dock battered by the elements, where ships are readied for their next voyage. Mock pulley systems inspire unique ways to stylise hanging pendant lights in the modern home.

➤➤ Subway tiles suggest a factory of nautical hardware, or the sort of rough-and-ready on-land diner where a fisherman or sailor eats his first home-cooked meal.

➤➤ Seek out sea art. Seafaring was once the most common form of transportation and, as such, its importance was expressed in art. Immortalised in paintings, the ship became a symbol of progress, fearlessness and power.

➤➤ Hunt out blankets and throws woven in a loose cable-knit that, as well as adding functional warmth, have the appearance of nets.

➤➤ Stack piles of vintage books with worn spines in all shades of blue as a homage to the colours that make up the ocean.

➤➤ Add sea-worn rope to almost any item to introduce nautical flair. For example, replace the hanging wire of a vintage bevelled-edged mirror with hefty rope to create an appealing juxtaposition.

Chapter 3

Islander

A LEAFY, WOODY SCHEME INSPIRED BY THE EARTHY ABUNDANCE OF A TROPICAL ISLAND

AND IT WAS GOOD TO BE
A PART OF THE WORLD
AND A WORLD OF ITS OWN
ALL SURROUNDED BY
THE BRIGHT BLUE SEA.

— *THE LITTLE ISLAND*, BY MARGARET WISE BROWN, 1946

Palm-fringed shores

→ **A tropical oasis, where the lush jungle forest and swaying palm trees give way to the sea.**

The islander theme takes the concept of a coastal holiday one step further, asking how you would exist if you were to live on a tropical island forever. With plentiful supplies from island plantations, create your hideaway beach hut from what is on offer around you.

DEEP FOREST

FRESH GREENS LEND A SENSE OF
VITALITY TO THIS TROPICAL MOOD
BOARD. Notice how the mix of textures begins from the
baseboard up, each layer adding further contrast and interest.
Geometric patterns in a block design have a definite tribal feel,
while botanical illustrations offer visual inspiration for fabric
designs. Textile edges are left raw and unfinished. Buttons,
beads and carved tribal artefacts have a natural unevenness,
offering a tactile experience. Shells reconnect the shore to
the sea.

Islander
(noun)

AN INHABITANT OF AN
ISLAND.

Island
(noun)

1. *A LAND MASS,* ESPECIALLY ONE
SMALLER THAN A CONTINENT,
ENTIRELY SURROUNDED BY WATER.

2. *ESPECIALLY* IN BEING ISOLATED
WITH LITTLE OR NO DIRECT
COMMUNICATION TO OTHERS.

ISLANDER
COLOUR PALETTE

Tropical greens (1, 2) reign supreme against light wood and sandy beige (3) tones; incorporating earthy base colours allows these verdant tones to really 'pop'. Ground the scheme with the inclusion of muted browns (4) found in textured barks and coconut shells, and the warm tan of well-travelled luggage (5).

→ SEEK OUT THESE ELEMENTS TO CREATE AN ISLANDER LOOK IN YOUR HOME.

➤ Lush tropical foliage ➤ Natural-texture wallpapers ➤ Pineapples ➤ Bamboo blinds ➤ Hula skirts ➤ Rattan furniture ➤ Hanging chairs ➤ Day beds (or other furniture you can easily lounge upon!) ➤ Shell mobiles ➤ Carved wooden furniture ➤ Leaf-shaped platters and plates ➤ Bamboo-handled cutlery ➤ Muslin lanterns ➤ Mosquito nets ➤ Terrariums (it's easy to make your own) ➤ Bamboo cloches (to repurpose as light shades) ➤ Pressed flowers and botanical illustrations ➤ Tiki masks ➤ Shark's tooth jaw casts ➤ Coconuts ➤ Tribal headdress and neckpieces ➤ Brass binoculars

CREATING AN
EVERYDAY RESORT

As a child I was always confused why, on school photo day, when we were all set up in front of the camera, the photographer would grin at us, abandon the usual 'Cheese!', and instead urge us to cheer 'Holidays!'

Now, as an adult, I realise why that simple word causes people to smile from ear to ear. The idea of a getaway from our everyday existence conjures up warm and heartfelt memories, instantly lifting the spirit and transporting us to a place where our breathing calms and hearts beat slower.

In Australia we're surrounded by ocean on all sides, so it's no wonder that holidays go hand in hand with bodies of water. We either escape to the edge, as far as we can go, where the land meets the sea, or cross the waters to venture further afield.

Regardless of where you live, how wonderful it would be to create an 'everyday resort', capturing the tranquillity of a coastal holiday within the four walls of daily life.

LAND TIME

Sailors were often given 'land time' when they arrived at their destination, giving them opportunity to explore the unknown wonders, and perhaps dangers, of the new land before them. As they recovered their 'land legs' after what may have been months at sea, many were no doubt happy to simply rediscover the pleasures of the earth. Others, however, as we know from historical letters, drawings and paintings, were on a voyage of discovery, recording every detail of their temporary new home, including the native flora and wildlife, as well as plant samples and specimens they had picked, trimmed, flattened and dried.

Imagine the exotic air and the thrill of the foreign for these sailors and seafarers: strange animals, alien languages and customs, and new flowers with intoxicating scents. Now imagine, upon the sailor's return home, his walls proudly displaying island souvenirs and gifts from his travels at sea.

Incorporate functional and decorative elements from your island sojourns into your everyday life, inspired by the natural beauty of the trees and the sea: tribal patterning in monochromatic hues influenced by foliage, feathers and fur; shells gathered and refashioned into garlands in the manner of island handcrafts; and spiky palm leaves laid flat and dried to create silhouette wall art.

A vintage hula skirt becomes the central inspiration for the palette of rich tropical greens used throughout this chapter. Notice the hessian band detail and the tan stitching as a complementary hue.

A simple whitewashed wooden
love seat fits neatly into the alcove of this bay
window, as though made for it. Layers of
tropical green create an inviting setting, with
cushions and fabrics in leafy green prints
adding comfort. A mosquito net is draped
whimsically from above, with simple bamboo
lanterns offering another point of interest.
A carved-stump side table feels right at home
here, with a collection of shells and organic-
shaped pottery in similar green tones
completing the look. Mock tile wallpaper is
rolled out to ground the set-up, its intricate
patterning mirroring the tangle of greenery
visible through the window.

This table setting is inspired by land time, as if a sailor-turned-botanist has set up his temporary work quarters in a linen tent on the island's shoreline. Here he lays out his latest finds to admire and analyse, using heavy bound books from the mother country to cross-reference his notes.

The linen curtains enclosing the tent are overlapped. Hung low over the circular table, a lantern hand-crafted from bamboo and the lightest of silks takes on an organic form.

On the table, glass domes display shell and plant specimens. Create your own terrariums by simply placing offcuts of succulents and cacti in shells to encase their roots. These hardy, water-wise plants only need a mist of water as a quick drink every now and then to keep them happy.

The island's lush green foliage is replicated in the batik fabric, casually thrown across the table as a landscape of patchwork designs, each inspired by nature itself.

Platters and plates in leaf motifs are reminiscent of botanical illustrations and hark back to a pre-industrial time, when communication came from the skill of hand upon paper.

Complementing the round table, the rattan floor mat is made up of smaller rattan circles, all working with the circular tops of the glass domes to give the setting a pleasing visual continuity.

An army-green enamel pendant shade hung from rope, teamed with a fold-out wooden stool with a simple striped canvas seat, suggests a temporary camp for exploring a new-found tropical island. Wallpaper with a palm tree motif is rolled out as a backdrop, and the kantha blanket, hand-stitched in similar colours and patterns, sits folded and ready to offer warmth to the voyager on their first night on the island.

Can you imagine a more tropical
alfresco setting in which to recline and relax?
This poolside corner cabana is purpose-built
with a raised platform large enough to hold a
king-size day bed. The thatched roof provides
shelter from the elements, while also adding
hand-crafted texture. A carved Balinese
window panel set in one of the sandy rendered
walls offers a glimpse of the forest beyond.
Take inspiration from the surrounding lush
greenery as the starting point for your textile
palette, then balance the hues with a warm
tone, introduced here with the spectacularly
large seashell.

LOFTY ISLAND
TREEHOUSE

Set the table for a tropical feast.
What exotic fruits and berries will you
discover around your new island home?
Take their organic forms as inspiration for
your table setting. Here the food cloches and
covers in semi-circular textured shells mimic
fruit husks.

Above the striking driftwood chandelier,
the vaulted ceiling is painted all-white to
emphasise the airy nature of this outdoor
room, with the balcony giving canopy views
into the lush vista beyond. This open-sided
space is a wonderful example of blending
interior and exterior architecture.

Maximise the proportions of a lengthy
dining table by creating a fabric table runner,
here in a geometric green pattern, that flows
down its entire length and cascades onto the
floor at each end. The hefty proportions of
the wooden furniture are counter-balanced by
the structure's solid support beams, giving a
hand-constructed aesthetic, connecting with
the magnificent tall trees outside.

Notice how the inclusion of a rug softens
this outdoor space, its simple striped hues
harmonising perfectly with the interior and
external setting, as well as the mix-and-
match cushions. As a fresh final touch, some
cut tropical leaves on the table bring the
island jungle into the home.

Light woods mix effortlessly with tropical greens. To the right, a vintage German teaching chart demonstrates a variety of ferns and sets the leafy tone, while the collection of seashells emphasises the coastal connection. On the chair a classic ticking fabric in green (rather than the more usual blue or red) mixes with a lattice-print linen cushion and a tactile ikat throw with worn fringing. All the green tones here – from lime green to bottle green – create a pleasant spectrum, balanced by the gentle wood hues and the vintage-paper tone of the fern wall chart.

Simple everyday kitchen items – such as the vintage milk jug, above, and cutlery with moulded bamboo-patterned handles – are both practical and decorative, and help turn meal times into magical island moments.

Farne

This room just begs you to take an afternoon siesta, don't you think? The light wood tones and vivid yet soothing greens all add to the inviting feel.

A mosquito net centrally draped over the bed creates a heavenly canopy, cascading onto a variety of soft linens gracing the bed.

The bed frame is impressive in scale, and the intricate carved wooden tile feature and whitewashed tone adds to its hand-crafted appearance. Notice how the inclusion of one cushion displaying a palm tree motif instantly transports the dreamy setting to a far-flung island. Taupe linens brought into the scheme balance the brighter colours.

A chandelier of wooden shards floats over the space, as if in homage to sea life. You could imagine it moving in the late afternoon coastal breeze, bringing refreshing coolness to the balmy evening.

The sliding louvre doors add to the impressive architecture and continue the appealing symmetry of the space. They are highly functional, creating privacy when closed, while allowing cooling sea breezes in through the panels.

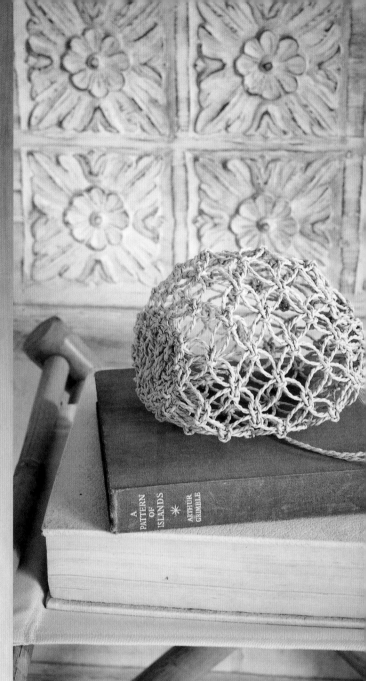

Recalling a traditional fold-out
fishing stool, this lightweight bamboo stool
can be easily moved around and used as a
plinth on which to display found items.

Even piles of aged books can be used as
temporary pedestals to display little treasures
upon. The more tarnished and yellowed the
pages, or threadbare the spine, the better!
Match such books in colour-coded piles, or
group them based on titles to delightful effect.

Who doesn't love the idea of an outdoor shower?
It's the perfect spot to wash the remnants of the day's
adventures from sandy feet before entering the home. Exposed
plumbing and the simplest of showerheads are all that is needed.
With its flaking paint and rusted fixtures, the reclaimed jetty
pylon dug into the ground, as though it has always been there,
becomes a sculpture referencing the nearby sea. Underfoot,
similarly rustic sleepers become a shower platform. A rendered
pure white wall shields the bather from the neighbours' eyes.

A bamboo cloche is hung by knotted rope as a temporary bedside pendant. The real purpose of such an item is to cover and protect delicate plant life, so it is ideal in this green-toned scheme.

Seek out vintage books with amusing titles to use as decorative pieces that tell a story. Here, *Voodoo Island* has a cover design that suits the mood and colours of the room and its title strikes an amusing note.

An ornate day bed beckons you to take an afternoon snooze. The carved wooden frame is suggestive of Balinese artisan markets where you might find one-of-a-kind treasures. Notice how the circular design of the cushion, created with stitched-on sticks, mimics the low-hanging pendant.

A bold splash of green on the inside of one shutter door breaks up any formality in the architecture of this building. Shutters help control ventilation and light into the home.

Seek out homewares and furnishings that have an organic influence. Here, a green chevron-stripe pattern and palm-leaf motif add to the feeling of a tropical oasis.

Step up onto this alfresco lounge area, where the wood decking has been left untreated to age gracefully from exposure to the elements. Overhead, a canopy is created from lengths of tree trunk that produce delightful shadows over the space, depending on the time of day and angle of the sun.

UPCYCLING & REPURPOSING

As you may have noticed, I'm not one for sticking to convention, especially when it comes to reimagining furniture pieces and putting them to new use.

There is one rule, however: the item should be the same height as the piece of furniture it is replacing, otherwise it won't be very functional or practical. Side tables and stools are almost interchangeable, along with any item that is around 45 cm (18 inches) tall. Stack crates or suitcases to this height; conveniently, these items also allow for extra storage within.

For a bed, you could layer wooden transport pallets to a height of around 60 cm (24 inches), including the mattress, to make it a suitable height.

Wooden cable reels are perfect for dining on if they're large enough — up to 75 cm (30 inches) tall should allow for comfortable seating. A cable reel that is around 40 cm (16 inches) high makes a unique coffee table.

TIKI TIME!

In Maori mythology Tiki was the name of the first man. The term evolved to refer to any large wooden or stone carvings made in a human-like shape, which were used to signify the entrance to sacred sites on the Polynesian islands.

Create a display of the finds from your tropical expedition. A large carved wooden mask in classic tiki style complements the smaller sculpture of a female villager. The leaf-patterned fabric draped as a wall covering introduces tan into the colour palette, reminiscent of languid sunsets, or the worn leather of a seasoned traveller's luggage. Mixed cushion coverings add tactile interest. A hand-carved wooden stool, organic in tone, doubles as a side table for a pile of books chronicling island adventures.

This kitchen exudes artisan workmanship. Designed and created by a crafter, the flaws in the wood are left exposed, even highlighted — note how the deep cracks contrast against the vivid green paint. The island bench has an impressive, heavy tone, as if carved from one massive tree.

The bench top is dressed with carved vessels with a similarly organic tone, displaying island fruits. The bouquet of mini pineapples makes a unique floral arrangement that is bound to draw attention. Befriend your local florist and ask them to keep an eye out for such rarities at the early-morning flower markets.

On the wall, a simple yet appealing pattern is stamped out in a soft-green pigment. A souvenir tablecloth looks far from kitsch here as its colours and motifs blend perfectly into the scheme. If you have a discerning eye and can weed out the tacky, you never know what you might find in souvenir shops. Vintage tourist items hold great appeal as they offer an insight into the aesthetic of another era, and a nostalgic glimpse into how we chose to spend our leisure time.

This bedroom has the relaxed feel of a tropical plantation-style home, an effect achieved through the white wood panelling and the low louvre window, which opens out onto the island greenery beyond.

Inside, rich tropical greens in leaf motifs and stripes delight the eye, accented vividly against the white walls.

I adore pendant shades hung low to the bedside, like this bold green wicker dome. They are functional for individual bedtime reading, and their proportion and scale when placed in this position really work. If you are building or renovating, suggest to your electrician you'd like to wire in similar lights. Even consider making the drop cords extra-long — you can move them around the space by looping them from hooks on the ceiling, for different looks and placements.

I love how this setting is so other-worldly. The exotic peacock-style wicker chair has been updated with a coat of vivid tropical-green paint, and rests upon a simple but wonderfully tactile sea grass mat that has a hand-crafted artisan feel. A side table is modelled from a raw wood trunk; upon it, a large shell holds whispers of the sea.

A lazy hammock rests on standby against a hand-crafted basket, ready to be strung up for an island siesta.

SEA GRASS MATTING

The manufacturer of this sea grass matting, so popular in the 1970s, once carried over twenty styles and designs. Nowadays there's just one variety on offer, but it makes for a cost-effective floor solution you can simply cut with garden shears and lay yourself. The texture isn't exactly plush, but it is perfectly practical for a beach shack, where sandy feet are the only ones that come through the door.

This simple table setting mixes
many impressive elements to tell a unique
story. Underfoot, a geometric, tribal pattern
is stamped out in striking green and white,
a colour theme that continues in the massive
pendant, hung low above the table and strung
up by rope; a simple stripe of green paint has
been applied to suggest a tropical air. The
industrial-looking chairs were formerly
school chairs, imported from the Philippines.
The untouched wall has an arresting patina
in natural tones, an effect softened by the
makeshift muslin blind, with bamboo rods at
each end. The raffia tasselled beach umbrella
suggests many sundrenched days of seaside
pleasure, every ounce of colour stripped dry
by the sun, wind, salt and sea spray. It rests
here against the wall, waiting to be put to use.

Along this wood-panelled wall, the
homeowner found just the right spot to mount
a handsome panel salvaged from a previous
renovation. It's a unique piece asking to be
hung and displayed with treasured mementos.
The hessian covering the wall panel earths
the tropical palette, the greens in the leaves,
botanical illustrations and treasure maps
playing delightfully against it. The jute floor
mat adds further textural interest.

The shell curtain that divides the spaces
has a lovely hand-crafted feel, while the
brown bamboo chair with winged armrests
invites repose.

I SAW A SHIP A SAILING...

This collection tells a story of tropical discovery:
brass binoculars on the look-out across the horizon;
a small boat ornately carved from wood and poised for adventure, resting upon tomes that retell stories of adventures;
a palm drawing posted to the wall documenting a new tropical find...

NATURALLY EXOTICA

Don't make a noise or they will dart away...
revered for their exquisite beauty, the elegant
egrets and flamingoes immortalised in these
paintings evoke images of an unspoilt island
paradise. The delicate pinks of the flamingo
feathers and lotus flowers are a perfect foil
for the lush green tropical foliage, creating
a fresh palette to draw ideas from.

Inspired by the bird paintings
opposite, this setting brings all their delicate
hues to life. A vibrant rendered wall makes
a lovely backdrop for the verdant tropical
foliage, the monstera leaves from the garden
help to blend the man-made setting with its
natural surrounds. A whitewashed timber
table is casually strewn with green linen
ticking as a make-do runner. But the hero
pieces are the vintage pineapple-back patio
chairs, left to rust into a weathered patina; the
seats are upholstered in old hessian sacks,
adding another earthy touch. Sea grass
matting is rolled out to help ground the
indoor–outdoor sensory mix-up.

HUNTING & GATHERING

Ebony black gives this scheme a tribal edge, the monochromatic hue suiting hand-crafted block patterns. Feathers, shells and coconut-husk buttons all add layers of interest.

In times gone by, the fine feathers of majestic island birds were valued for their intrinsic beauty and used for personal adornment, as the neckpiece mounted on a delicate stand shows. With its cut-shell and beaded collar, it displays a wonderful symphony of natural textures. Such previously hard-to-find pieces are now more readily available as decorative homewares (you might even choose to wear them on occasion).

The formality of the flock wallpaper hanging against the wall falls away when you identify the subject matter, and becomes instead a quirky homage to the most tropical of fruits, the pineapple.

The earthy palette maintains interest through the mingling of textures and tones. The grain of the wall, constructed from a stack of wooden sleepers, becomes a textured backdrop, while the bolted-on cladding balances the scale and weight of the solid wooden chair, softened by a black cushion embellished with coconut-shell buttons.

A sea-battered wooden sleeper becomes a shelf built into the architecture of this home. Upon it, a still life celebrates hunting and island crafts – an ebony-stained decorative mask resting next to a shark's jaw, the teeth still pointy enough to cause injury. A small chandelier hand-crafted from shells further connects this island home to the sea.

Layered textures bring to life
this striking black and wood scheme.
A woven rug creates the base texture,
which continues in the seat cushion of
the high-backed chair, covered simply in
a stamped hessian sack – using similar
colours and textures develops the subtle
palette. A carved wooden side table holds
a gloss-black pineapple sculpture for a
touch of whimsy, along with a trio of
fan-like leaves that have been dried
out and sprayed black.

Overhead, a spiky round wicker
pendant has a wonderfully organic look
– a prime example of how to take your
cue from the textures and forms found in
seaside nature and incorporate them into
a timeless design. With raw edges that
spin into an urchin-like protective
armour, this pendant looks thoroughly
modern and individual.

MORE ISLANDER STYLING IDEAS

➤ Indoor palms create a green oasis. Add hanging planter pots with delicate ferns, or wall-mounted staghorns, to create your own indoor rainforest. Or hang palm fronds above your dining table as a simple yet eye-catching centrepiece.

➤ Work pineapples and other tropical fruits into floral displays. Long gymea lily leaves, birds of paradise and flat tropical leaves create a lush mini-rainforest in a vase. A simple stylist's secret: a squirt of hairspray adds extra sheen to plant foliage.

➤ Seek out Hawaiian broadcloth and hessian base fabrics in neutral hues and strong open weaves. The stiffness of these textiles suggests a hardy, island-ready purpose.

➤ Sea grass wallpapers are reeds woven into beautiful tactile papers, every bit unique — no two sections are the same, unlike mass-produced decorative patterns. A thin line is visible between each loom; it's an effect you would try hard to avoid when using normal wallpaper, but sea grass proudly displays its mismatched joins, saying 'I'm unique! No two parts of me are ever the same.' Just as in nature.

➤ Use tribal-inspired headpieces and necklaces as décor items. The most elaborate is the juju hat, a circular creation consisting of hundreds or more feathers. It can be found in every colour of the spectrum, from natural white to vivid hues. When hung flat, it transforms into a striking wall piece.

➤ If you are planning a new home, draw inspiration from island nations. Interconnecting pavilion-style pods, popular in Indonesia for example, offer laid-back coastal living.

Chapter 4

Bohemian

A FREE-SPIRITED
LIFESTYLE INSPIRED
BY THE COAST AND EXECUTED
IN A CORAL KALEIDOSCOPE.

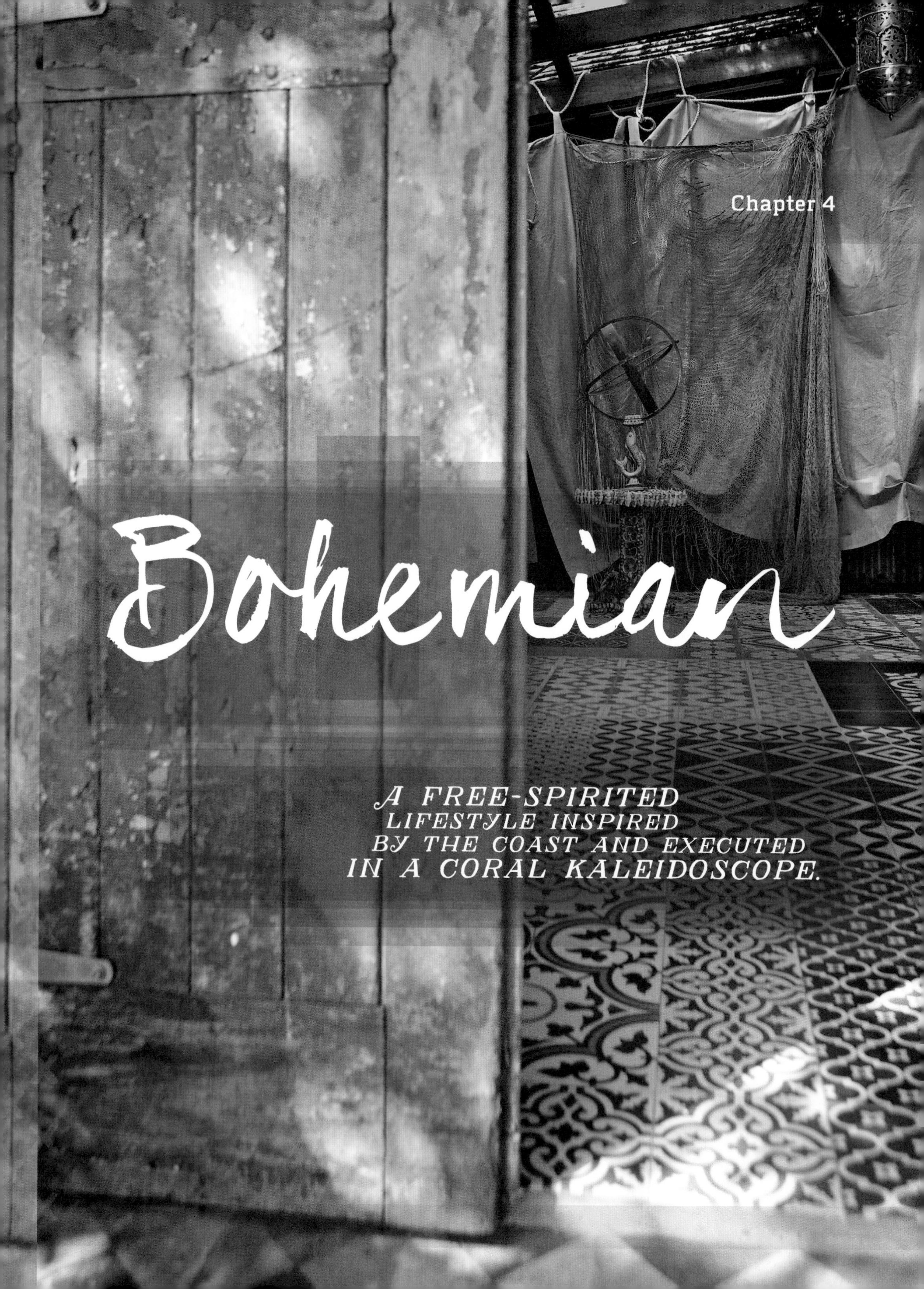

WE ARE ALL WANDERERS ON THIS EARTH.
OUR HEARTS ARE FULL OF WONDER, AND OUR SOULS
ARE DEEP WITH DREAMS.

– GYPSY PROVERB

Colourful adventures

→ The word 'bohemian' is thrown about a lot these days in many design mediums, from interiors to fashion; it has even been affectionately shortened to 'boho'.

Due to its occasional overuse, I find myself drawn to the term 'gypsetter' — an amusing combination of the initially seemingly contradictory labels of 'gypsy' and 'jetsetter'. Upon consideration, however, there are parallels in the lifestyle of both, each roaming the globe in search of the unique and inspirational. This blend of gypsy/jetsetter adds a dash of luxury to the nomadic gypsy life, better reflecting the lavish tone of the style. Both are drawn to spaces of warmth and personality and, above all, to satisfying their highly individual desires and tastes.

Bohemians perfectly capture the free-spirited nature of the coast, which goes hand in hand with a relaxed beach culture lifestyle from decades past.

SOFT AND PRETTY

A BEACH SUNSET IS THE STARTING POINT FOR THIS PALETTE, IN WHICH THE COLOUR CORAL is a prominent hue. Treasures from the ocean floor, such as colourful pearly shells, are a wonderfully apt inclusion in an eclectic collection. Carry the inspiration through into beaded and dyed fabrics and ribbons; detailed patterns emerge that are exotic in tone, such as mismatched Turkish tiles and ikat textiles in an array of colours and designs. This is the most feminine of the schemes, so mermaid iconography is a fitting element.

Bohemian
(noun and adjective)

1. *A NATIVE* OR INHABITANT OF BOHEMIA.

2. *UNCONVENTIONAL* BEHAVIOUR OR APPEARANCE, ESPECIALLY OF AN ARTIST. A PERSON WITH RELAXED CONDUCT.

3. WITH FEW *PERMANENT TIES.*

BOHEMIAN
COLOUR PALETTE

A burst of colour reminiscent of undersea gems... turquoise (4), teal (3) and burgundy (1) all mingle to maximum effect in this aesthetic. The deep tones of each are suited to heavier fabrics such as velvets and heavy-loom rugs. It's also the most feminine of the coastal palettes, where dusty pinks (5) emerge, inspired by coral hues and summer sunsets. Aged gold (2) echoes the metallic sheen of fish scales and adds a touch of relaxed glamour.

SEEK OUT THESE ELEMENTS TO CREATE A BOHEMIAN LOOK IN YOUR HOME.

➤ Moroccan lanterns and tea glasses ➤ Lotus-shaped tea-light candleholders ➤ Intricate carved wooden screens and side tables ➤ Ikat and embroidered fabrics ➤ Turkish tiles ➤ Persian rugs ➤ Crocheted hammocks ➤ Leather ottomans ➤ Fans ➤ Paper parasols ➤ Genie bottles ➤ Bongo drums ➤ Brass teapots ➤ Tassels and fringing ➤ Feathers ➤ Delicate doilies ➤ Crocheted cloths ➤ Woven lampshades ➤ Floor cushions ➤ Beaded curtains ➤ Jewellery as décor ➤ Large clam shells ➤ Clusters of pink barnacles

LIVING ON THE EDGE

Bohemians appear within many cultures, from the Parisian art community and the flamenco-obsessed Spanish gypsies to early twentieth-century Hollywood royalty. First by foot, then by gypsy caravan, the bohemians gravitated away from the conventional society of their time.

Each of the sub-cultures listed above had an artistic impetus to work away from the mainstream. Bohemians have always sought out creative solitude, and often found it on the shores of some little-populated island or coast; the ultimate spot for relaxation and inspiration.

These days the bohemian aesthetic lives on, albeit less radically and more intertwined with a stable life path. Journey to Byron Bay in New South Wales, for example, and you'll find a modern-day family tribe that seeks out a different pace of life to that on offer in any big city. Similarly, Brooklyn is a creative outpost to the main streets of New York. What especially pleases me is seeing the successful artistic output that comes from living on the edge. The modern-day bohemians continue to be active participants and leaders in their creative fields from their reclusive wonderlands, connected these days thanks to email and the internet.

It's almost a self-exile from the mundane of the mainstream. As such, it becomes all about escape, a different pace, and a search for inspiration. What evolves is a unique aesthetic that mixes new cultures with trinkets discovered on worldly travels.

Such a 'gypsetter' style often incorporates Indian fabrics and patterning, which is perhaps not surprising as gypsies themselves originated in India, way back in the ninth century.

They were a tribe that travelled by foot and gradually spread throughout Europe, so you can understand how the melded bohemian look emerged from these overlaps of culture.

A broad style, the bohemian aesthetic touches on many design mediums, including fashion. Designer Yves Saint Laurent would reach for paisley as a signature print, and immerse himself in a reclusive lifestyle in Morocco. In the 1990s John Galliano would pile layers of embellished fabrics on models on the Milan catwalks as a reference to that early twentieth-century golden era that holds eternal appeal.

The mix-up of styles and cultures has always been at the heart of the bohemian outlook. This can be replicated in the modern abode by mixing aesthetics and patterns. A communal notion is reflected inside bohemian spaces; rooms are decorated for multiple purposes, where one large space with a low-to-floor sleeping area might double as a casual area in which to lounge and entertain.

Original gypsy homes such as tents, yurts and other temporary dwellings are still popular today, especially for the youth that congregate for music festivals, often by the coast. Such events seem like modern-day installations paying homage to the bohemian traveller's roots.

Haven't you ever wanted to escape
outdoors on a balmy summer's night... to go
down to the water's edge and set up camp
under the stars for the evening? Here the
free-spirited residents have done just that,
only indoors. Sure to delight the young and
young-at-heart, this simple tepee is formed
from a pyramid of birch branches, enclosed
by a delicately embroidered cloth that is
exquisitely highlighted against the sandy,
patchy patina of the walls.

   Inside your private oasis, mix and match
ikat rugs, pillows and throws to create layers
of bohemian comfort. An ornately carved low
side table is the ideal piece on which to set up
a brass fondue set. It's the simple pleasures
that delight here.

BOHEMIANS
AND THE BEACH

Most recently it was the culture shocks in the 1960s that spawned a new generation of mainstream bohemians: surfers and surf culture.

As a society, when new freedoms emerged, so too did the means to achieve it — in the form of the modern road trip. Volkswagen Kombi vans became the contemporary gypsy caravans of choice, building on the earlier American motorcycle culture. It was youth's escape-pass from the prescriptive path their parents had laid out for them.

The nomadic experience became commonplace, and went hand in hand with surf culture as the ultimate expression of freedom. In the film *Big Wednesday*, for example, a modern-day tribe of blond-haired surfer boys travels around America in search of the perfect wave, in an almost religious pilgrimage, finding an alternative existence, carefree and idealistic.

As is the case with many pivotal cultural movements, bohemian style gradually moved into the mainstream; even the fresh-faced Beatles went on their own 'hippy trail'. For me the most personal example is that of my parents, who are as far from gypsy as you could get, packed it all up in the last year of the 1970s, before I was born, to travel around Australia in an orange Kombi on their own personal pilgrimage — a surf-inspired road trip. Other Australians went even further afield, with London luring an entire generation of free-spirited teenagers.

The myriad colours and patterns in this pair of patchwork harem pants offers a vibrant starting point for an interior colour scheme.

FASHION AS INSPIRATION

If you don't know what kind of colours or patterns to include in your home, the answer is simple: open your wardrobe. This will give you an instant idea of the kind of aesthetic you are personally drawn to.

What do you immediately see hanging on your racks? All black? Patterns? Varied textures? Are the fabrics shiny or dull?

By writing down your answers, you've straightaway named a few of your favourite things that can easily be translated into interior solutions. Colours that are predominant in your wardrobe can easily be matched to paint swatches, and fabric styles can be matched to a heavier upholstery version as a starting point for your own personal interior style.

A high-back single chair is made more comfortable with cushions aplenty. Flock velvets mix with intricate embroidery and a fragile Indian sari has been turned into a cushion cover. Such a combination sums up the bohemian aesthetic: a mix of styles where more is more.

A groundcover of layered Turkish carpets creates a warm welcome. Instead of competing with the already-busy wall cladding, the carpets actually add to the layered visuals of the space. Look for similarly coherent hues when working with such a lively backdrop.

Consider how you place your items and what will be the statement piece. It's a similar concept to creating a still life of smaller objects on a shelf, but in this instance real furniture pieces follow the same rules of scale and positioning.

Here, the focal points are a trio: the chair, a bongo drum (upcycled into a side table) and a vintage parasol. The umbrella doubles as a backdrop to the coral display, linking back nicely to the core coastal theme. Each piece is overlapped to highlight its most attractive feature; for example, the parasol is unfurled in full bloom behind the chair, rather than just left rolled up and hidden.

Set on delightfully rustic sea-green floorboards,
an exotic bohemian platter holds a collection of tusks,
suggesting adventures in far-flung lands across the oceans.

Fitting enough for Miss Havisham to take
possession of, the Victorian-era ship model is the hero piece
of this room, ornately beaded and threaded in fabulous colours,
with cotton strands, dust and cobweb-like wisps. It is so delicate
that even the anchor once attached now floats astray.

The ship has come to rest against a cluster of barnacles on
a rustic Indian-inspired side table, the battered colours of which
blend into the paint-flaked wall, which itself resembles a cloudy
sky that the ship is sailing against.

A waft of ikat fabric hung casually over the door frame
enhances the exotic colours and patterning of the room.

This antique Indian coffee table, reminiscent of an old wooden rum cask, holds wonderful appeal. Low to the floor and with its circular shape giving all guests equal status, it's the perfect spot to gather cushions and sit comfortably among friends sharing travellers' tales and refreshments.

A futon mattress is rolled out to suggest communal sleeping quarters in this beach shack, which looks as if its walls have seen many vibrant coats of paint over the years. The temporary bedding is made appealing by the pile-up of cushions and textiles in an array of colours and textures.

Coral pink with gold embroidery mixes wonderfully with a Prussian-blue velvet, its gold accents balanced by the other textiles in the scheme. A draped crocheted fabric in antique linen tones calms the space.

A low seat, nowadays better for looking at than sitting upon, has been stripped back to its hessian underlining, its inner springs protruding – an effect softened by the ornate cushion and costume Indian headdress, and the lovely feminine fringing on the crocheted lampshade. A gypsetter pattern emerges in the red fabric draped across the floor as a covering. Such a clash of patterns is typical of bohemian style, where a lively dance of colour and pattern creates literal layers of visual interest. Here, all the variety works together, balanced by the rustic basecloth of the chair. Sitting against the wall, a magnificent old clam shell brings the coast into the room.

COLOUR: BASE VERSUS BOLDS

Bohemian is one of the most colourful coastal schemes, but even
with its richness of patterns, textiles and contrasting hues, it's
far from an assault on the senses. This is achieved by a couple
of styling cues. First, all the more elaborate pieces – cushions,
wall hangings and other decorator items – are usually small in
size. The backdrop to these selections is kept as a simple neutral
base tone, preferably with a rustic patina. Such earthy contrast
both balances and enhances the more ornate choices, for
example letting feminine fabrics 'sing', but in doses measured to
the scale of the overall setting.

   Second, observe how most of the bolder colours are never
used at full volume; what is evoked is a muted 'not-quite-bold',
perhaps because the pieces themselves are vintage and have
lost some of their original vibrancy over time. Touches of gold
may slip into the intricate patternings, but even these metallics
look far from glitzy, offered up in tarnished tones.

This homeowner took inspiration from the pattern on a bohemian silk shawl like the one in the image, left. The paisley print is magnified en masse over the walls as a mural, below. Balance the oversized scale with oversized objects, such as the clam shell and hefty rope tassel draped over this chair. The intricate carvings on the wooden chair back continue the graphic floral theme.

This window is adorned simply with a fringed shawl, the warm golden tones of the silk contrasting pleasingly with the battered ocean-blue wall paint. The floral pattern in the scarf is mirrored in the dried hydrangeas, as well as the decorative glass panels in the window, which may well open out onto a coastal horizon. The crucifix has been lovingly encrusted with shells gathered from the ocean's shore.

STYLE INFUSION

This scenario is a perfect example of a cross-chapter styling solution. Through the main window, the jungly tropical bamboo nods back strongly to our previous Islander exploration, but the hut itself features a bohemian colour palette. Here the hanging tribal masks are painted in richer, bolder hues than the natural tones used in Islander style. The couch throw creates a striking basecloth on which to pile a range of mismatched cushions and fabrics in ikat and embroidery.

A primitive carved stool, used as a side table, displays an impressive shell as a salute to the sea; the duo work together to create a wonderful sculptural form. This is an ideal nook for an afternoon siesta, as the sun sets low and casts inviting shards of light through the bamboo blind.

This repurposed boatshed sits at the base of a waterfront property, its panelled doors literally opening out onto the sea. The exterior of the dwelling has been engulfed by vibrant green tangled vines over the years, enhancing its gypsy-caravan feel. Open to the elements on one side, it's an informal space for leisure and pleasure. The functional trappings of such a boatshed — fishing nets, ropes, a hammock — become decorative features within the scheme. The muted soft green wall blends in with the natural world outside the shed, and is a perfect base colour for all the contrasting textiles and patterns within, setting the oversized fiery paper lantern ablaze. A day bed has been built into the room's architecture, immediately changing the purpose of the space. The bamboo lounge chair adds a leisurely beachside feel.

Red and green traditionally scream Christmas, but tweaking the palette to a cooler green and a warmer red produces an entirely different effect. The result is a calming but warm bohemian palette.

A copper bowl with an intricate embossed peacock pattern creates a palette for the gypsetter scheme. Rich plum tones are offset by the burnished-gold detailing of the spoon. The olive green linen adds to the eclectic mix, while the pearly blue shell harks back to the sea.

You can't help stop and admire a unique item of furniture such as this hand-painted Indian cabinet, delighting the senses with its warm sunset tones. Even though it is ornately patterned, it is far from showy, as the finished patina is quite flat and muted. An ikat wall hanging in golden chevron stripes adds zigzag flames to the green wood-panelled wall.

Use thoroughfare-furniture pieces such as console tables and buffets as your own mini museum of curiosities. A bohemian installation assembles here with a trio of miniature wicker peacock chairs. Play with the scale of objects by placing the largest object first and working your way down. Shells and coral establish a coastal connection, while a small Tibetan bell offers a touch of Zen. The unexpected inclusion of a porcelain bird completes the setting and stops the collection looking too themed.

This bedroom ticks so many boxes for me. All the eclectic elements are there. The aged green wall panelling instantly suggests a beach shack, the afternoon shadows on the wall adding a moody darkness. In contrast, a rich, warm coral and tarnished gold palette emerges in the bed linens and hanging fabrics, the rumpled patterns all mixing together in pure gypsetter fashion. Rustic oars and a rope necklace reference the ocean.

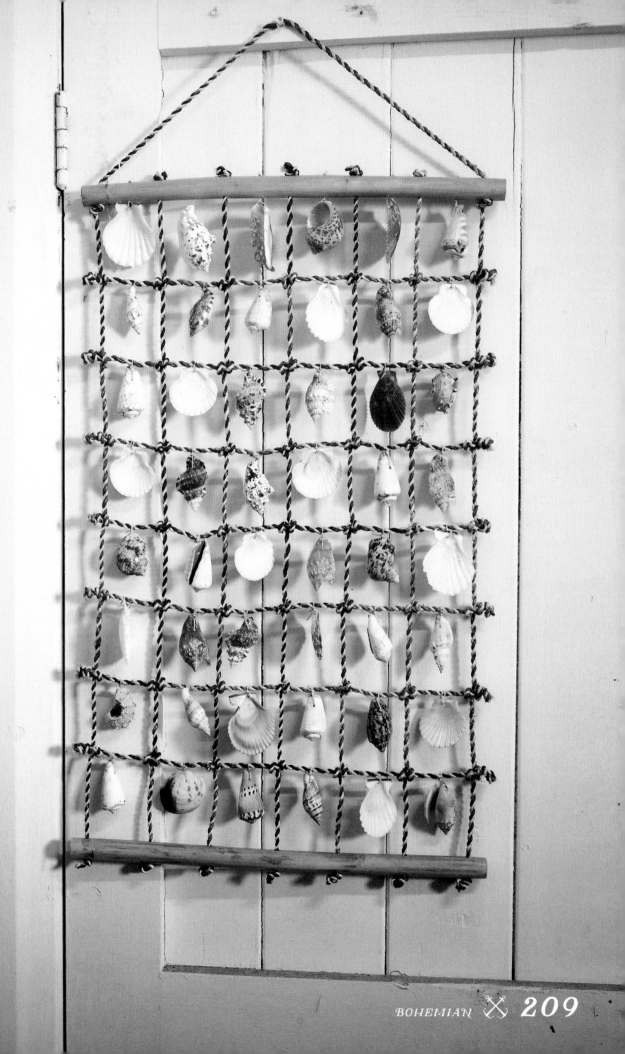

A warm afternoon glow streams into this living space, adding further warmth to the wooden interior. The choice of neutral brown lounge upholstery lets the large furniture piece sink back into the setting, allowing the vividly patterned cushions and ottomans to take centre stage. An embroidered Indian elephant on the coffee table begs to be picked up, while a guitar sits ready for a round of communal folk songs as day turns to dusk.

DREAMCATCHERS

Dreamcatchers are made up of a circular hoop with a web woven across the centre, and are decorated with sacred items such as feathers and beads. Native American mothers made these to protect their infants and filter out bad dreams. Eight points in the web design are symbolic of a spider's legs, referring to Asibikaashi, also known as the Spider Woman in Native American culture, and believed to be a protector of children. Dreamcatchers have featured in the adopted iconography of generations of gypsetters.

On a rustic wooden sideboard, a collection of decorative pieces makes an interesting vignette of treasures acquired from worldy travels. A tin deer gets reworked with the inclusion of a real antler wound in stripes of colourful wool, finished with a bold green feather that links with the delicate dreamcatcher hanging against the wall. The Moroccan teapot almost resembles a genie lamp.

Near the entrance of this home
an intricately worked Ethiopian cross rests
theatrically on a bentwood chair, suggesting
the eclectic curios to be found further within
this dwelling.

Host to a riot of colour, this ornate day bed has had its carved timber frame whitewashed to erase any sense of formality. Playful patterns are used to opulent effect — the intricate embroidery on these mismatched cushions illustrating flowers, fanciful peacocks and paisley designs. An indoor plant adds an organic element mimicking the folksy flourishes in the fabrics. A vintage birdcage becomes a display enclosure for a pink-toned shell, a fitting link to the sea.

In Turkish and Mongolian, 'yurt' simply translates to 'home'. Its tepee-like design was developed as a portable dwelling by nomads of Central Asia thousands of years ago. The circular form is not only appealing but symbolic, leading the eye to a central crown pattern overhead; this centre emblem would be passed down through generations, even though the yurt itself may have been rebuilt over time. Layers of insulating sheep wool traditionally covered the self-supporting tent structure.

Some gypsetters have adopted the yurt as a modern-day portable abode; it makes perfect temporary accommodation for a music festival, for example. You can easily create your own mobile retreat – capture the mood by decking out a yurt or tent with all forms of plush comforts, referencing a medley of styles, from the vibrant fabrics of the original gypsies to a relaxed beach look of beaded shell curtains.

The structural circular wooden latticework provides an interesting backdrop for the bedroom setting in this modern cloth-covered yurt. The floor is piled with Turkish rugs in warm tones, providing an inviting passage underfoot. The bed is strewn with linens in contrasting plum and orange tones, the artisan patterns mixing to wonderful effect, and the orange hues adding an almost Buddhist-like serenity. An eye-catching trio of elaborate umbrellas filters the natural light from the skylight above, giving the space a warm glow.

A small wooden dressing table is set up with folksy items and adornments, ready to add the finishing touches to your outfit.

This table setting reminds me of an underwater dive to a colourful coral reef: clusters of spiky coral and bubbled barnacles in blushing hues, its palette of faded pinks and azure blue, all brought further to life with a sprinkle of tarnished gold.

The fan is a feminine motif that offers a visual link back to the flamenco gypsies who pioneered bohemian style. The vintage crocheted tablecloth, on which are laid an assortment of linens that have been over-dyed in brilliant hues, adds a further sense of femininity to the setting.

Tea-light candleholders and embellished Moroccan tea glasses suggest the far-off and exotic. Don't be afraid to use a mix and mismatch of crockery and cutlery to create a similarly relaxed, rummaged gypsy appeal. Platters and plates often have an ornate appearance, but in a setting such as this they are far from formal.

This patchwork floor of elegantly patterned tiles has a hypnotic effect that sums up the bohemian aesthetic of mixing old and new, feminine and rustic.

The amazing mosaic flooring, and the entrancing texture of the hammock – strung up like a fishing net, resplendent in the marine hues of some mythical sea creature – set the space for the seashell-encrusted pedestal. It glistens and glows in pearly sheens of pinks and aquas, all playing against each other as though plucked from an underwater wonderland. Perched on the pedestal, a rustic sphere is a sculptural focal piece, proudly supported by an upturned fish.

Like altars to the sea, these unique shell-craft creations are superbly displayed against the clean white wall. Each shell has aged over time, retaining just a remnant of its original pearly gleam; their muted aspect blends well with the darkened timber doors of the carved Indian buffet underneath. The bouquet of pink and golden flowers, crafted from individual shells, adds a soft, feminine appeal to an otherwise woody scheme, balancing the bright pompom garland that drapes onto the richly hued Aztec rug.

The lavish engravings on this wooden console find a subtle echo in the textures of the shell-covered lighthouse table lamp, a loving tribute to seashore life. A dark-stained Eastern icon and bright tropical blooms suggest gypsetter travels to coastal islands and back.

A day bed is casually covered in mismatched cushions, setting off the random patterns in the distressed wood panelling behind. Small paper lanterns add a festive touch to the everyday setting.

A fantastical rattan bedhead fits into the 'peacock'
family of furniture, so-called because of their resemblance to
a peacock's display of feathered beauty. Spreading over the bed,
a patchwork of folk prints are stitched together, complemented
by richly patterned cushions and a lotus-shaped table lamp on
the wooden side table.

At the end of the bed a beautiful carved bench seat holds a
collection of folksy painted boxes and trinkets that suggest a
gypsetter's favourite pastime: travel. Open a box to find
hand-collected shells, which can be made into original and
individual jewellery pieces; the sea often creates the perfect
opening to thread such pieces together into unique designs.

MORE BOHEMIAN STYLING IDEAS

➤ Drape scarves and tasselled shawls over furniture ends: a true sign of a bohemian's blend of fashion and interiors.

➤ Take this a step further and pin a large sari to the wall as a delicate bedhead. Ornately carved decorative screens suit a similar purpose and exude a feminine flair.

➤ Wicker and rattan sculpted into unique furniture finds such as high-back peacock chairs are perfect for the bohemian look. Bring them up to date with a coat of paint, rustically whitewashed or with a pop-coloured hue.

➤ The almost-forgotten crafts of macramé and beading are rediscovered by a new generation. Seek out hanging planter pots and decorative wall hangings — vintage finds, if you are lucky, or modern creations in fashionable coloured threads.

➤ The bohemian existence is a creative one, but also a leisurely one. The most enriching or expressive ideas may come from an afternoon siesta on a crocheted hammock hanging beside a beachside abode, so source relaxed furniture pieces that inspire artistic thought-time.

➤ Lay a wall in mismatched Turkish tiles, each one handcrafted and painted so no two are the same. Such a mosaic is a graphic example of the individual spirit of this aesthetic.

Chapter 5

Endless Summer

COLOURFUL STYLING
DRAWING UPON
NOSTALGIC SEASIDE
HOLIDAY MEMORIES.

A VACATION IS
HAVING NOTHING TO DO
AND ALL DAY TO DO IT IN.

– ROBERT ORBEN

Sunny shores

The most colourful of the coastal decorating schemes, this style recalls those long, carefree days of youth and warm, golden summers from days gone by.

Patterns and palettes once considered kitsch find fresh new forms, tugging on the heartstrings and harkening to a simpler time.

FADED GLORIES

THE MOST VIBRANTLY JEWELLED OF THE COASTAL MOOD BOARDS... BUT NOTICE HOW EACH HUE IS A FADED VERSION OF ITS ORIGINAL LUSTROUS SELF. Over time, worn by the elements, layers of paint have flaked and paled. Holiday souvenirs, postcards, happy snaps and mementos are all joyously collaged here. Seductively coloured lures and other fishing paraphernalia please the eyes of both landlubbers and fish. Coral pieces hand-painted with food dyes re-establish an underwater wonderworld on land.

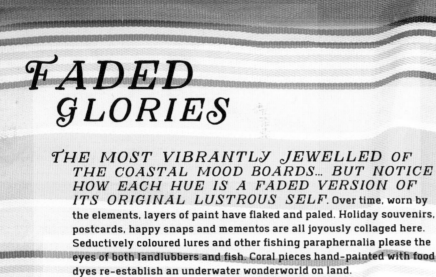

Endless summer
(slang)

1. A SEEMINGLY EXTENDED DURATION OF THE WARMEST SEASON, WHEN REMINISCING AT A LATER DATE.
2. THE TITLE OF A CLASSIC SURF MOVIE.

ENDLESS SUMMER
COLOUR PALETTE

The sizzling tones of this palette recall trips to the beach kiosk and the kaleidoscope of sorbets and lollipops on offer. Flamingo pink (1), canary yellow (5), mint green (4), a coral hue (2) and ocean blue (3) fit the liquorice-stripe scheme. However, all are presented in a slightly faded hue, like that of a once-vibrant holiday postcard. It is the washed-out tones that tie the seemingly contrasting colours together so successfully.

To visually communicate a concept through a colour palette, try something outside the square: dip vintage tourist spoons into sample paint pots and lay them side by side for a unique vision of how the different tints will look next to each other and the story their combination has to tell.

SEEK OUT THESE ELEMENTS TO CREATE YOUR OWN TAKE ON AN ENDLESS SUMMER LOOK IN YOUR HOME.

Vintage postcards Felt tourist flags 1960s patio furniture
Striped canvas Colourful fishing lures Retro beach towels
Surfboards Striped umbrellas Paper umbrellas Vintage vinyl (for the covers as much as their tunes) Deck chairs Plastic strip door curtains Souvenir-shop salt and pepper shakers Original ice-box coolers and cordial bottles Garden ornaments, such as flamingoes
Don't forget the garden sprinkler, essential on a hot afternoon!

HOLIDAY CHARMS

So many of us have fond memories of childhood family holidays, packed into a car alongside siblings. It seemed like a never-ending road trip to get to the seaside destination, punctuated with cries of, 'Are we there yet?'.

This chapter's aesthetic has its tongue firmly planted in its cheek. The aim is to entice a sense of thoughtful nostalgia and amusement at the way we once spent our leisure time.

I still love getting out on the open road with the stereo pumping. Passing sleepy little coastal towns full of unchanged charm and character, I sometimes find it hard to keep my eyes on the road, drawn in by the breathtaking rural scenery, roadside fruit stands and, my personal favourite, the country motels. Next time you're driving to a remote seaside town, where a caravan park or camping spot beckons, notice the pastel-hued motor inns dotting the freeways. Their kitsch aesthetics never fail to delight. It's almost as though there's a

competition among motel owners as to who can display the brightest plumage of colours on their painted brick façades, and who can light up their neon 'Vacancy' sign in the gaudiest retro font with the most fanciful sea mascot. The names themselves often sound like exotic cocktails.

In Australia any long journey is often broken by the bizarre sights of our peculiar obsession with enormous iconic sculptures: the 'big Merino sheep' or the 'big prawn', the 'big banana' or even the 'big beer can'. We like it larger than life, moulded in fibreglass and impaled on a stick – preferably in the middle of nowhere. I guess it breaks up the never-ending road trip into smaller chunks of enjoyment. I imagine it's a similar effect to the scale of signage at Las Vegas, Times Square or Piccadilly Circus ... except our landmarks are spaced hundreds of kilometres apart.

Imagine a travel brochure from yesteryear come to life as an interior setting in your home. But it's not merely a retro re-creation presented here – each styled scenario mixes both the vintage holiday with the new. The contrast presents a fanciful way of spending those long summer days.

Objects from the past are offered up in weathered tones, preventing the kitschiness from looking too overblown, and casting the past in a soft and sympathetic light.

Some holiday items remain timeless and perenially appealing, no matter what generation reinterprets them as their own; a striped umbrella, a colourful body board or melting ice creams all play a part in our collective summer vocabulary.

The Gold Coast

SOUTHPORT
MAIN BEACH

SURFERS PARADISE

BROADBEACH

MERMAID BEACH

MIAMI

BURLEIGH HEADS

PALM BEACH

CURRUMBIN
TUGUN
BILINGA
KIRRA
COOLANGATTA
TWEED HEADS

WORLD
OF WALL ART

Against plain white wall panelling,
an ever-growing and changing artwork emerges
in this home. By simply sticking and pinning
vintage holiday postcards in a random group,
it is easy to create an appealing collection that
works as a mass artwork because of the common
shapes and colours.

A pair of old wooden deck chairs, in what would once have been rich red and sunny yellow, are testament to many days of enjoyment in the summery outdoors. Resting alongside, fishing rods await their next outing. Reminiscent of a canvas from a caravan, or a kitchen from an earlier era, a tartan pattern is rolled out in pastel tones. A blue enamel fan sitting on one of the chairs speaks of warm summer days, while a vintage wall thermometer charts the rise in mercury. The pineapple print cushion in canary yellow adds a contemporary burst of colour.

SHADES OF SUMMER

Pull up an original patio chair, updated
with a spray of teal, and join the backyard party.
A record player pumps out tunes from another
era; seek out vintage record sleeves for their retro
cover artwork. The striped beach towels mimic
the canvas on the impressive umbrella, which
provides much-needed shade. Plastic strip door
curtaining adds colour and movement, keeping
unwanted flying insects outdoors.

Make yourself a mocktail in retro glassware
– complete with a paper umbrella, of course. The
cockatoo garden ornament looks right at home in
this scheme.

This original fibro beach shack has been
invigorated by being painted a fresh green all
over, with contrasting white trims and a fuchsia
pink roofline, paying homage to the era in which
it was built. It certainly is noticeable from the
street! But the bold colour choice seems an
appropriate one here, holding its own against the
clear blue summery sky.

Nothing typifies Endless Summer
more than a wall of longboards, lined up
in sorbet colours against a mint-green
privacy screen. Wooden decking and
outdoor furniture are left to weather
gracefully through exposure to the
elements; the fresh colours of the sunny
cushion and striped towel seem even
brighter by contrast. A classic black
and white awning completes the
quintessential beachside cottage look.

This sunny bedroom scheme tells a summer story. The golden walls provide the backdrop for a holiday-inspired collection. A much-loved surfboard is assembled as a bedhead, the scale of a board perfect for such use. The bed is dressed with simple striped linen, its fringed edge reminiscent of a beach umbrella. The original 1950s cooler box is an unusual round shape, but makes a great bedside table. A cockatoo lamp is an eye-catching piece, especially when lit. On the wall, a felt tourist flag evidences holidays from times past.

HOT FOOD
ICY COLD
DRINKS
ICE CREAM
DELICIOUS
FLAVOURS

Canary yellow, sky blue and crisp white create a classic coastal palette, one that is also a popular choice for brightening beachside bathing boxes. These colours immediately transport me back to childhood days spent at the local public swimming pool. Many of these pools remain unchanged since the 1960s, with stencilled diving blocks and cement grandstands, their sun-washed, pastel-coloured hues complementing the ripples of the crystal-clear blue water, like a David Hockney painting of Hollywood sun and sky against a summer patio landscape.

The mosaic floor tiles in this beach shack remind me of those on the bottom of a swimming pool, often spelling out words or the number of the swimming lane.

A pineapple-print wallpaper evokes a simpler time, with the motif manifesting again in the base of the vintage table lamp. The old tasselled shade is updated with a lick of paint, the yellow stripes resembling a bright kiosk awning.

Blue is an unexpected choice for a pineapple, but therein lies the whimsy of this set-up. Do you remember how, to make food appealing to children, it was often re-created in a fanciful colour? Consider the variety on offer at the pool kiosk: rainbow paddle pops, tutti-frutti icy poles and other bright-coloured ice creams that left a blue stain on your tongue well after the initial enjoyment.

Borrow slogans from a poolside kiosk for your next informal gathering; make a sign pointing to your drinks station or finger-food table, heralding 'Icy Cold Drinks' and the like. While you're at it, consider serving up mini ice-cream cones as a novel dessert.

Wrap a circular side table in colourful nylon rope to resemble a wharf-side reel of rope. Imagine the same idea executed with a sea-worn rope; this would create an entirely different effect.

GIVE ME A SIGN...

By both seaside and poolside, you'll find graphic inspiration that you can work into your endless summer scheme. Safety signs such as 'No Diving' or 'Deep Waters' hold amusing appeal.

Consider taking photographs of signposts and their unique fonts, from the hand-painted to the mass-produced, and then using sections of the image as artwork, or applied as designs on fabrics for cushions. The human eye quickly fills in the gap when sections of words are missing, so there's no need to literally spell things out.

Here, a faux 'No Vacancy' sign is displayed to great effect, as a salute to kitsch roadside motels. The lesson here: stop and take another look at signs you would normally pass by. Reinterpret them in new ways to add a unique, nostalgic and whimsical flair within your home.

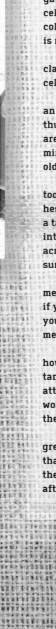

This fibro beach shack embraces its inherent kitschness by being painted flamingo pink all over – the ideal hue to complement a summer sky. The sloped rooflines reflect the architecture of another era, and are suggestive of a roadside motel that has never been updated.

String up a temporary clothesline at your next outdoor gathering and hang decorative fabrics as a backdrop to your celebration. Here a flamingo design in the same pop-hued colourway as the building and sky sets the mood; the motif is repeated in the lawn sculptures that stand guard.

Patio furniture in powder-coated metal takes on a classic lattice-back form, recalling Hollywood Hills celebrity mansions from days gone by.

Even the green of the sculptural yucca plant becomes an integral part of this palette. As a self-confessed brown thumb, I'm a fan of hardy, water-wise succulents that are virtually unkillable. Create your own portable miniature cacti garden by planting spiky specimens in old soup cans.

Introduce natural fibres to stop the scenario looking too plastic — here a striped sisal rug grounds the look, and hessian sacks emblazoned with colourful iconography add a tactile texture to the mix. One hessian sack is upcycled into a floor cushion, while another sack drapes casually across the table as a runner. Other cushions sport a summery striped liquorice-allsorts design.

Keep an eye out in thrift shops for discarded tourist mementos, such as the salt and pepper shakers here. Even if you've never been to a particular holiday location yourself, these quaintly kitsch pieces instantly evoke memories of summer holidays.

Have you ever looked closely at a fishing lure? See how much work has gone into each design, illustrated in tantalising hand-painted detail to lure sea life onto the attached hook. The colourful spray-painted designs are worthy of table decoration I think, but consider removing the pointy ends for safety.

Seek out original old cooler boxes, such as the 1970s green esky under the table opposite — an insulated chiller that holds ice cubes galore and keeps bottles frosty cold in the heat of summer. This one has retained its colour, even after decades of being dragged to the beach and back.

This antique deckchair has seen so many days by the seashore that the canvas is almost threadbare from use. It's an ideal seat to while away time and wait for the next bite; the hand-painted cushion offers inspiration as to what to use for bait. A heavy rope is moulded into a whimsical lamp base, a suitably nautical touch.

An original 1940s caravan is a sandcastle on wheels. Renovated to suit its original era, a palette of sunny yellow mingles inside and out with classic bottle green. Striped canvas, used on the awnings, deckchair seating and umbrella shade, complete the retro look. A tartan picnic rug in similarly sunny hues is the perfect spot to set up for a day of leisure or activity.

Pop inside the caravan for a bite of afternoon tea. The table is set in classic gingham and mismatched crockery; the buttery yellow walls induce an instant craving for freshly baked scones with jam and cream. Felt flags were once popular tourist items, demonstrating where the traveller had been; see if you can build a collection on your own travels. The pink cockatoo-print cushion introduces a modern vibe.

Every nook and cranny of this caravan is used as functional storage space. The owner has filled each cupboard with original items, from the tiny kitchen cupboard to a fold-out wash basin, where vintage toothbrushes still nestle in their original wrapping. Camping and caravanning were seen as rugged, manly pursuits, so these finer amenities for ladies made all the difference in persuading 'the missus' to embark on a holiday adventure.

Brighton Beach, just outside
Melbourne, Victoria, was a favoured
seaside spot at the turn of the twentieth
century. Following a European trend,
these small bathing boxes were built along
the shoreline for private use.

The simple structures are made of a
timber frame with weatherboard cladding
and corrugated-iron roofing.

Each of the 82 bathing boxes lining
Brighton Beach has its own individual
colour scheme – an ideal starting point
for your own summery palette.

It is the ultimate celebration of fishing prowess to mount your biggest catch on the wall, for all to see. Here, a mock catch becomes a delightful hanging spot for assorted fishing floats paraphernalia. The multi-coloured door strip curtain seems to beckon you inside, into what could only be imagined as a suitably kitsch interior...

MORE ENDLESS SUMMER STYLING IDEAS

➤ The classic old fibro-clad beach shack is often a little run down, but alive with a kaleidoscope of clashing thrown-together colours, in which mismatched hand-me-downs mingle with newer gadgets.

➤ In this scheme, the almost-clichéd comes into play. Retro seabird illustrations that might have once featured on a fifties dad's summer shirt now appeal as cushion designs.

➤ Heavy canvas fabrics are made for outdoor use and exposure to the elements. Stripes in candy-hued colours evoke summer all year round.

➤ Classic timber Adirondack chairs offer perfect reclining opportunities on the porch of your private beach shack. For a more mod option, try an Acapulco chair made of plastic tube woven into a similar tilt-backed design.

➤ Vintage surfing and fishing paraphernalia hold enduring appeal, speaking of skills and memories passed down the generations.

➤ Bring the outdoors in: plant hardy succulents and spiky cacti in individual upcycled vessels, such as empty tins, to create an interior desert.

➤ Borrow from the style of yesteryear, when a cockatoo statue might proudly welcome you to an entrance hall. Re-evaluate what is kitsch and what actually evokes happy holiday memories.

➤ Drape the branches of a tree or a washing line with colourful fabric to make a canopy under which to laze the afternoon away.

Thank you

Where to begin with my thank yous? Before the process of this, my first book, unfolded, I knew it would be a massive journey. What I didn't realise was how many people would become involved and dedicate their time and energy to supporting me and the *Sandcastles* vision.

Johan and his lovely family: Nouha, thank you for lending me your husband for many months. Johan is an expert photographer, my travel companion and a dear friend. He makes my work look like an instant masterpiece and the experience is always effortless and enjoyable.

The team at Murdoch Books, especially publisher Diana Hill, who believed in me from the moment we met. Jane and Sophia for making me sound as eloquent as possible.

Sarah, my designer, for artfully creating layers of beautiful interest in the design of the book.

My family. My late father, Stephen, who encouraged my first steps towards finding a publisher. My mother, Rhonda, sister Melinda and her husband, Justin, who are endlessly supportive.

And friends, who never tired of my endless 'Show and Tell' updates about the book.

LOCATION, LOCATION

We were lucky that the owners of almost every door we knocked on responded warmly when invited to be part of this book. They gave up their time and granted access to the gorgeous homes they have created, and then let me turn everything upside down with my own styling! Thank you to these homeowners:

Frances, Avalon
Jennifer, Winmalee
Katrina, Avalon
Merryl, Palm Beach

Locations, also available for holidays

Beach Villa, Palm Beach, Sydney, NSW
This owner's holiday home is magnificently decorated, as you would expect: she spent 15 years running an interior design store on Sydney's northern beaches. Her signature style of relaxed décor, natural textures and a strong but muted palette is used throughout the home. We were drawn to the tropical aesthetic of the exterior and the alfresco spaces, which have a lush plantation look. From the master bedroom you can step out to enjoy a dip in the 10-metre lap pool. www.stayz.com.au/accommodation/nsw/sydney/palm-beach/119724

Blue Belle Bondi, Sydney, NSW
Hidden discreetly in the top floor of a 1960s beachside block of units is this delightfully decorated holiday home. The all-white wall panelling creates a charming backdrop on which sea-worn life rings and oars are hung to wonderful effect. However, this is far from a museum to the sea that you can't touch. Instead, visitors feel instantly at home to enjoy both the interior décor and the natural wonder and tourist offerings of famous Bondi. Designer Kathy never disappoints with the little luxury touches, such as a claw-foot bathtub that you would never expect in a building of this era. www.bondiholidaylettings.com

Contemporary Hotels
I remember the first time I stayed at the Medusa Hotel in Sydney's eastern suburbs: it opened my eyes to the world of boutique hotels, which weren't common in Australia at that time. No wonder proprietor Terry Kaljo was named one of the '25 People who changed Sydney'. At Contemporary Hotels she has rounded up a selection of stylish designer beach houses, villas and apartments, mainly in Australia but now also around the globe. www.contemporaryhotels.com.au

Gidget Goes to Culburra, Culburra, NSW
Named after the 1960s fictional surfer girl, this is one property you won't ever drive past by accident. This original fibro surf shack has had its entire exterior painted in eye-catching flamingo pink, while the interior has been architecturally reconfigured to make the most of natural light and open-plan living. Out the back the former boatshed is now a separate sleeping and bathing area. This is a unique and relaxing place from which to experience the south coast of New South Wales and is only a few metres from the beach itself, which is proudly dog friendly, like the house. www.gidgetgoestoculburra.com.au

Lemon, Lime & Bitters, Culburra, NSW
If Gidget, above, is the iconic 'pink' house of Culburra Beach, Lemon, Lime & Bitters is the 'green' one. This is another original fibro beach house that has been given a new lease of life; you'll find all the modern trappings in the kitchen and bathroom while you enjoy the unique decorative style. Owner Anne has taken to the walls with colourful murals, all painted in relaxing tones. The garage is converted into a convenient accommodation annex, separate to the main house. Kids will love the massive backyard. www.stayz.com.au/accommodation/nsw/south-coast/culburra-beach/25027

Snapper Lodge, Newport, NSW
Snapper Lodge was top of my locations list for this book. This converted boathouse has been lovingly decorated over the decades: its walls are covered in massed nautical iconography, such as lighthouses and fishing reels. The location is romantic: step out of this quaint hideaway onto the private jetty and watch the sun set over Sydney's Pittwater. Then fall asleep to the sound of gentle waves lapping beneath your bedroom. www.contemporaryhotels.com.au/beach/snapperlodge

Toraja Luxury, Byron Bay, NSW
Toraja is situated just out of town so it has a country feel, looking out over the grassy hinterland to the coast. It wasn't until we visited for the photography shoot that I realised how appropriate the luxury title actually is; this is a home of grand proportions that beautifully displays the craftsmanship of builder Damien Connellan. Host Sarah has executed a soothing and interesting set of interiors with one-off furniture pieces, such as carved Indian consoles and unique accessories. Plenty of room for up to three couples. www.torajaluxury.com.au

Trelawney Farm, Mudgee, NSW
This 1880s dairy farm is now a little piece of stylish serenity among the vineyards of inland New South Wales. Kathy Collins from Urban Splash created the holiday property with her usual design flair, reconfiguring the floor plan into spacious open-plan living areas filled with atmospheric spaces, industrial-inspired furniture and decorated with vintage collectables. Given the size of the property, it's perfect for a wedding or for a dual-family getaway. www.trelawneyfarm.com

Historical places

Vintage Caravan Hire, VIC

I almost squealed with glee when an original 1947 caravan rolled into a waterside car park in Frankston, Victoria, for us to photograph. The owners are only the third in its history and have affectionately named it 'The Don', after the original Victorian company, Don Caravans, that produced this design. For owner Alan his growing business goes hand in hand with a personal passion — he owns at least a dozen vintage motor homes in varying states of restoration, each one a lovingly created time capsule available for hire for a unique escape. After our shoot, The Don was setting off as honeymoon accommodation. www.vintagecaravanhire.com.au

Yurt Creations, Bangalow, NSW

The dome-shaped, tepee-like yurt has a traditional nomadic heritage, but in modern times it has become popular for camping and music festivals. I knew Byron Bay would be just the place to find one, and, of course, Tiffany and Sul from nearby Bangalow run a business called Yurt Creations, specialising in the hire, set-up and even custom building of these structures with their impressive criss-crossed wooden beams. On their property is a yurt that can be rented as accommodation if you are visiting. www.yurtcreations.weebly.com

Brighton Beach Bathing Boxes, VIC

The iconic Brighton Beach bathing boxes are a strip of 82 simple wooden shoreline structures, based on the European bathing huts of the Victorian era and famous for their brightly coloured facades. www.brightonbathingbox.org.au

Fort Scratchley, NSW

For some of our photography we took occupation of an ex-military fort for the day. Set high between the gorgeous beaches of Newcastle, New South Wales, Fort Scratchley was originally built to protect the coastline from invasion. Now it has to be the most picturesque vantage point of my hometown, giving a panoramic view over the ocean and city. We were drawn to the old barracks buildings, once used as accommodation for marines. Both spaces and a modern, multipurpose function centre are available for hire. www.fortscratchley.com.au

Port Stephens Shell Museum, NSW

A favourite spot of mine, Port Stephens is only a 45 minute drive north from my hometown but it seems like a world away. The flat, clear waters of Shoal Bay stretch to nearby Corlette, where you'll find a hand-painted 'Shell Museum' sign sitting among a row of unassuming suburban houses. Step inside the front room and discover a quaint space overflowing with the owner's treasures, collected from the shoreline over many years. Needless to say, I left with arms full.
92 Sandy Point Rd, Corlette NSW 2315 (02) 4981 1428

Ray's Museum of the Sea, NSW

Johan and I came across this treasure trove a few years ago when we were on our way to nearby Kingscliff. In the small coastal town of Chinderah, Ray's barn of nautical paraphernalia stands out on a street corner. We were drawn in by the rustic lobster pots hanging above the doorway, but never expected to find what we did: two levels filled to the brim with maritime wares, ranging in style from rustic fishermen, to tiki and shell craft, for exhibit, hire and purchase. Ray is someone who lives his coastal passion everyday.
www.facebook.com/pages/Chinderah-Bay-Antiques-Museum-of-the-Sea/149447215096992

The designers

Debra Cronin Design

Debra's grand Woollahra House in Sydney was a 'must-visit' location at the top of my shoot list. It has featured many times in interiors magazines and as a backdrop for fashion shoots, so the three-storey, purposely dilapidated terrace house just oozed inspiration. Debra, an interior designer, uses the crumbling mansion as a rustic canvas to display a Victorian aesthetic, with an eclectic array of furniture and decorative collections, including an impressive wall of birdlife taxidermy. The ground floor kitchen and dining area hosts frequent culinary get-togethers, artfully named The Underground Bite Club. A lover of coastal style, Debra has also recently completed an extensive renovation, Culburra House, in her sought-after signature style. www.debracronindesign.com www.biteclubhouse.com.au www.culburrahouse.com

Jatana Interiors

Sonya Marish has created her own range of reproduction floor tiles, inspired by rare antique designs discovered on her travels. The varying styles are all executed in a matt ceramic finish that gives a modern feel against the ornate patterns. Sonya's showroom is on the family property in Federal, rural New South Wales, in a fascinating barn-like structure with a show-stopping floor covering: a mosaic-like design made up of various patterns mixed together as one. Sonya's designs are popping up more and more in magazines and quality commercial fit outs around Australia, mixing modern with old-world style. www.jatanainteriors.com.au

Kathy Collins, Urban Splash

Kathy was a contestant on the Australian TV show 'The Renovators' and now shares her expertise and unique design flair through Urban Splash, her Sydney-based property development company. She and her builder–husband specialise in renovations that maximise the potential of any style of home, with hundreds of completed projects under their belts. I adore Kathy's eclectic styling aesthetic, which mixes in one-off vintage finds as the final touch. www.urbansplash.com.au

Lisa Madigan

After noticing artist Lisa's gorgeous Kangaroo Valley, New South Wales, home in many interior design magazines over the years, I was thrilled to finally visit. We bonded over a similar beachcomber aesthetic, and Lisa also creates changing displays of found objects. The overall 'greige' tone of the home is an aesthetic that continues into the paintings she creates in a light-filled studio on site. Lisa is proof that you can't take the beach out of the girl: when asked what's her favourite part of the rural village she calls home, she answered 'the beach', even though it's a good 50 minute drive away! www.lisamadigan.com.au

Rory Unite

I had the pleasure of studying with Rory at NIDA. I dreamt up the theatrical props and he had the hands-on skills to turn those ideas into reality. It was wonderful to be reunited with him at the Palm Beach home Rory has created with his in-laws. I wasn't surprised to learn that this now Bali-based artisan crafted most of the furniture and fittings himself. His style is a blend of modern organic: think bar stools with carved wood seats on chrome bases. www.roryunite.com

Walter Barda Design

If there's one man who knows about Australian coastal home design, it's architect Walter Barda: he has crafted more than 30 properties on Sydney's northern beaches alone. Each abode features his organic influence, with caves and trees as motifs of inspiration. His own Palm Beach weekender is a delightful update of an original coastal dwelling, executed in earthy hues and an inviting, eclectic and personal style that chronicles his travels with partner, Tom. www.walterbardadesign.com

Stylist's little black book

Auld & Grey

I've been doing the antique shop trail in my hometown since I was skipping classes in high school, but when I stumbled across Jenny Auld's treasure trove of vintage goodies I knew I had found a kindred spirit. Jenny peddles an eclectic mix of styles with a heartfelt aesthetic, from rustic country furniture to original industrial hardware. We shot a best-selling magazine cover in one of her cavernous retail spaces a few years ago; she has an eye for uncovering rare objects with rustic beauty that appeal to a wide audience. Always worth a visit: you never know what you may find.
www.facebook.com/pages/Auld-and-Grey-antiques-and-collectables/225518767489672

Book Luxury Locations

Location scout Deanne and I had many phone conversations on the exact nature of modern coastal style, as she had so many properties that may have suited the brief. From Hamptons-inspired to tropically landscaped to homely and rustic, she never failed to offer more locations than we possibly had time to visit. Rounding up the premier homes for events, photo, product, film and TV shoots is what she does best. She's always on the lookout for new properties, too.
www.bookluxurylocations.com.au

Crab Apple Vintage

Boy, did I get excited when this store suddenly popped up on my morning coffee route. Having sourced an eclectic mix of authentic vintage and industrial pieces, such as enamel pendants and rustic trestle tables, the team at Crab Apple Vintage also upcycles items such as lockers, ingeniously turned on their sides to become entertainment cabinets. Even better news: they hire anything in-store for events or photo shoots. While I was writing this book, I visited weekly to search out those hard-to-find finishing touches.
www.crabapplevintage.com.au

Major & Tom

This is a stylist's wonderland of crockery and cooking utensils, colour-coded on shelves throughout the warehouse space in Sydney's inner-west. Chances are, whatever tabletop item you need for your next shoot you'll find it instantly and easily in this stash of styling treasures. Pop upstairs for table linen and cutlery in every material imaginable.
www.majorandtom.com.au

Pure Locations

Testament to the power of the internet, location scout Michelle co-ordinated our shoot with homeowners in New South Wales while based in Queensland. Michelle makes the process easy and stress-free, and with over ten years' experience, her expertise is obvious, demonstrated by the calibre of homes she has rounded up. www.purelocations.com.au

Seasonal Concepts

Ken Wallis lives by the motto above his shopfront entrance in Sydney's Redfern: 'Delight the eye, cheer the heart'. This cavernous space is filled with rustic wares that exude personality, from industrial-inspired pieces to natural curiosities. Fresh blooms greet you with colour and fragrance. As curator and shopkeeper, Ken always has that special piece on hand to add instant personality to an interior space.
www.seasonalconcepts.com.au

The Establishment Studios

When I first took a tour of The Establishment Studios in Melbourne, I knew I had found somewhere special. There's magic in the air as natural light filters into the different spaces available for photographic shoots — each with its own personality of textured and painted walls. Step into the large warehouse and you're greeted by a wall of chairs in every shape, colour and style imaginable. Around the corner are furniture items, fabrics and props, all with a distinctive rustic and vintage edge: it's a stylist's heaven. It was no surprise to learn the studios were set up by one of Australia's best, Glen Proebstel. www.theestablishmentstudios.com.au

Products, retailers & inspiration

Armadillo & Co

I adore this rug company for their natural and tactile designs.
You'll see many of their woven creations featured in these
pages. Handmade in India by talented artisans, the creative
process is evident in every design. But it's their simplicity that
resonates with me; from the crocheted, circular, doily 'Marigold'
design that has fast become an iconic favourite with local
interior designers, to the coastal-inspired, striped 'Nest
Awning' in duck egg blue, their wares are unlike anything else
on offer in the marketplace. www.armadillo-co.com

Bandhini

Bandhini Homewear Design is proof of my belief that a cushion
can change an entire room. Each of their pillow covers is a work
of art, hand-crafted in India and inspired by trees, cocoons,
shells and seeds. The results are unique detailed textiles in
natural fibres. This Australian family business extends its arms
globally while having an ethical consciousness at its core.
www.bandhini.com.au

Bonnie and Neil

Not since artist Ken Done captured the colourful spirit of
Australia in the 1980s has there been such a design celebration
of our natural wonders. Bonnie and Neil create hand-printed
cushions, tableware and bedding featuring botanical motifs in
bold hues. Their unique plywood wall tiles in contrasting
geometric patterns define their combined artisan and modern
practice. www.bonnieandneil.com.au

Empire Furniture Newcastle

A favourite local store in my hometown, Empire Furniture
Newcastle has an ever-changing, massive warehouse showroom
full of eclectic wares. Owner Moyna Longworth's unique
offerings include furniture and decorative accessories, ranging
in style from contemporary, French and modern Asian to one-off
hardwood pieces. www.empirefurniturenewcastle.com.au

Empirical Style

When I was on the hunt for caged light bulb pendants I found
makers Empirical Style, who put together each ensemble to
personal specifications. Choose online from a variety of
fabric-covered electrical cords and cage shapes, which are then
custom-sprayed to your colour preference. Add an old-
fashioned Edison bulb to complete the look. I also adore their
hanging charts of botanical and scientific illustrations that
exude old-school personality. www.empiricalstyle.com

Escape to Paradise

Sacha Alagich's cushion range has been built around a tropical
textile design that has become much sought-after in Australia
in recent years. The effortless style of the botanical prints
comes from their soft colour palettes; the look is contemporary
and carefree. Most recently the range has expanded to bamboo
tableware, continuing the aesthetic of every day being a
'holiday at home.' www.escapetoparadise.com.au

Fabric Traders

Simone Georgette is my go-to girl for colourful print fabrics —
chevron, stripe or tropical, she always has an option in every
colourway imaginable. You might recognise some of her
imported designs, including Tommy Bahama, through the book.
I appreciate the quality of the textiles on offer: heavier weaves
suitable for outdoor use. Check out the remnants section of her
website for some last-chance finds. Add to this, always reliable,
prompt delivery to your door and what more could you want?
www.fabrictraders.com.au

The Family Love Tree

This retailer burst onto the scene a couple of years ago, offering
ornate wicker peacock chairs in every possible colour. They've
since grown to include other furniture items: lighting and
textiles that all have at their core the same colourful, nostalgic
charm. If you see a magazine spread featuring a piece of ornate
rattan furniture in a block bold colour, the chances are that it's
from them. The Family Love Tree are always evolving and
expanding their colourful core range.
www.thefamilylovetree.com.au

Have you met Miss Jones?

It seems this Australian design business goes from strength to
strength, with their offering of unique homeware designs
constantly expanding. Central to their range are well recognised
white bone china lamps and ornaments in intriguing shapes,
from squirrels to seahorses. Their vase range in contemporary
yet organic forms is particularly special, offering a variety of
on-trend colour options to mix and match. But it's the whimsy
of the designs themselves that never fails to delight.
www.haveyoumetmissjones.com.au

Online

Hermon & Hermon

Contemporary furniture, artwork and accessories all created with an artisan quality — no wonder Hermon & Hermon has such wide appeal. Their organic-inspired lighting range of tactile pendants that resemble birds' nests and fish scales are a perfect example of their style. www.hermonhermon.com.au

KAS

I'm drawn to KAS for their colourful, embroidered textile designs in cushions and bed linen, often with a bohemian spirit, which are updated each season. Add to the mix tactile throws, available at large department stores. Their unique designs offer an instant update to any interior space, especially bedrooms. www.kasaustralia.com.au

Porters Paints

The renowned Australian boutique paint company is known for their water-based, environmentally aware products. Their colours are pigment-rich and lustrous. Founded by Peter Lewis, the range also extends to designer wallpapers and, my favourite, the speciality finishes, which allow you to easily achieve an appearance of instant rust, zinc or iron through liquid forms. www.porterspaints.com

Safari Living

This retailer's online store of colourful and unique designer homewares and accessories follows the mantra of 'everyday luxury'. Safari Living has a stock list of international design brands, such as Missoni and Marimekko, and is also a stockist of Scrapwood wallpapers. These delight the eye with the illusion of wood textures, from dark timber to whitewashed simplicity. www.safariliving.com

Sanbah

I've had the pleasure over the past couple of years of working on the window displays of one of Newcastle's largest surf stores. Visit Sanbah for surf hardware, fashion and even surfing lessons. Oh, and the store's eclectic interior that mixes raw wood veneer with Turkish mosaic tile counters was designed by yours truly! www.sanbah.com

Sparkk

If a fanciful fabric or wallpaper catches your eye in the book, there's a good chance it's a Sparkk design. The Rysenbry family are long-standing interior industry experts and are embracing new textile technologies with this latest venture. I love their unique Australiana illustrations of waterbirds. Each design can be custom-produced in your own colourway. www.sparkk.com.au

Bright Bazaar

My current morning ritual is checking my blogs and Instagram over coffee. I love seeing that, while I've been asleep, the other side of the globe has been busy creating, tweeting and posting. This is one of my favourite finds, from the other side, offering a kaleidoscope of colourful interiors. www.brightbazaarblog.com

Lost at E Minor

I've enjoyed contributing to this pop culture hunting website over the years. They have offices in New York as well as Newcastle, New South Wales. www.lostateminor.com

The Design Files

These guys source the best creative home tours from Australia and beyond. They are a daily inspiration and feature crisp photography. www.thedesignfiles.net

Plumeria Coastal Home

Symantha Manauzzi's online store has been delivering a taste of the tropics right to your door reliably for many years. Browse a collection of Caribbean-inspired homewares and gifts, all hand-picked with an eye for the unique and the luxurious. Sam recently branched out to share her coastal finds on a lifestyle blog dedicated to the style. www.coastalhome.com.au

Published in 2015 by Murdoch Books, an imprint of Allen & Unwin

Murdoch Books Australia
83 Alexander Street
Crows Nest NSW 2065
Phone: +61 (0)2 8425 0100
Fax: +61 (0)2 9906 2218
murdochbooks.com.au
info@murdochbooks.com.au

Murdoch Books UK
Erico House, 6th Floor
93–99 Upper Richmond Road
Putney, London SW15 2TG
Phone: +44 (0) 20 8785 5995
murdochbooks.co.uk
info@murdochbooks.co.uk

For Corporate Orders & Custom Publishing contact Noel Hammond,
National Business Development Manager, Murdoch Books Australia

Publisher: Diana Hill
Design Manager: Hugh Ford
Designer: Sarah Odgers
Editorial Manager: Jane Price
Editor: Sophia Oravecz
Production Manager: Mary Bjelobrk

A cataloguing-in-publication entry is available from the catalogue of the National Library of
Australia at nla.gov.au.

ISBN 978 1 743361078 Australia
ISBN 978 1 743361085 UK

A catalogue record for this book is available from the British Library.

Colour reproduction by Splitting Image Colour Studio Pty Ltd, Clayton, Victoria
Printed by C&C Offset Printing Co Ltd, China

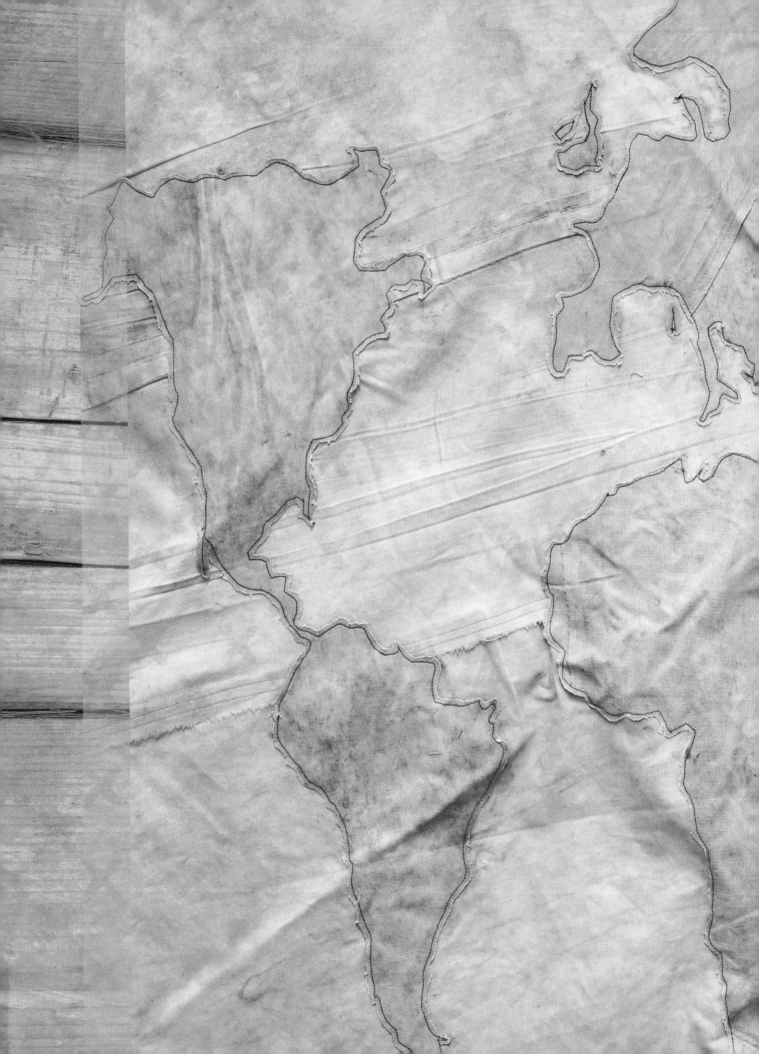